David Hume, Josiah Tucker

A brief essay on the advantages and disadvantages which respectively attend France and Great-Britain

With regard to trade

David Hume, Josiah Tucker

A brief essay on the advantages and disadvantages which respectively attend France and Great-Britain
With regard to trade

ISBN/EAN: 9783337131791

Printed in Europe, USA, Canada, Australia, Japan

Cover: Foto ©Suzi / pixelio.de

More available books at **www.hansebooks.com**

A BRIEF ESSAY

ON THE

Advantages & Disadvantages

WHICH RESPECTIVELY ATTEND

FRANCE

AND

GREAT-BRITAIN,

WITH REGARD TO

TRADE.

By JOSIAH TUCKER, D.D.
DEAN OF GLOUCESTER.

LONDON:

PRINTED FOR JOHN STOCKDALE,
OPPOSTE BURLINGTON-HOUSE, PICCADILLY.

MDCCLXXXVII.

Advertisement.

THE desire of receiving information in respect to the commercial treaty with France is, at present, so prevalent, that the Editor of the following sheets thought he could not perform a more useful service than by publishing intelligence, which appeared to him to be disinterested, and therefore satisfactory.

The first of the following works is a tract of that celebrated commercial writer Doctor Tucker, dean of Glocester, which is now reprinted from the third edition in 1753; and which, being written with a quite different purpose, may reasonably be supposed to contain the candid sentiments of a very competent judge on an interesting subject.

The second consists of three discourses, by

by that great master of political reasoning, Mr. Hume, the historian; being,

I. His Essay on the Balance of Trade;

II. On the Jealousy of Trade; And,

III. On the Balance of Power.

As this treaty has been discussed under two heads; first, as it affects our COMMERCIAL SYSTEM; or, 2dly, our POLITICAL POWER, the Editor humbly hopes, that every reader will receive ample information from Dean Tucker, as to the first, and the greatest satisfaction, as to the second, from Mr. Hume. With these hopes, the Editor submits both to the candid perusal of the reader.

THE INTRODUCTION.

ALL commerce is founded upon the wants, natural or artificial, real or imaginary, which the people of different countries, or the different classes of inhabitants of the same country, are desirous, in defect of their own single abilities, to supply by mutual intercourse. If this commerce be carried on between the inhabitants of the same country, with the growth or manufacture of that country only, it is called *Home Consumption*, which is so far serviceable, as it preserves the several professions and stations of life in their due order, as it promotes arts and sciences, with a rotation of industry, wealth, and mutual good offices between the members of any community. For these reasons, traffic, merely of this kind, is of great importance, though it neither increases nor diminishes the public stock of gold and silver.

But Providence having intended that there should be a mutual dependance and connection between mankind in general, we find it almost impossible for any particular people to live, with tolerable comfort, and in a civilized

civilized state, independant of ALL their neighbours. besides, it is natural for men to extend their views, and their wishes, beyond the limits of a single community, and to be desirous of enjoying the produce or manufactures of other countries, which they must purchase by some exchange. Now this intercourse with other nations is called *Foreign Trade*. And, in the exchange of commodities, if one nation pays the other a quantity of gold or silver over and above its property of other kinds, this is called a *Balance* against that nation in favour of the other. And the science of gainful commerce principally consists in the bringing this single point to bear.* Now there can be but one general method for putting it in practice;

* This is spoken with respect to the *ultimate* balance of trade. For in reference to the *intermediate* balance, it doth not always hold true. A trade may be beneficial to the nation, where the imports exceed the exports, and consequently the balance paid in specie, if that trade, directly or indirectly, is necessary for the carrying on of another more profitable and advantageous. But then it is to be observed, this trade is not beneficial, considered in itself, but only as it is relative and subservient to the carrying on of another. This is the case, with respect to the greatest part of our trade to the Baltic, and the East-Indies: they are instrumental in procuring a balance elsewhere, though, properly speaking, disadvantageous in themselves. Which brings the matter to the point from whence we set out; viz. "That the science of gainful commerce consists, " *ultimately*, in procuring a balance of gold or silver " to ourselves from other nations."

practice; and that is, since gold and silver are become the common measure for computing the value, and regulating the price of the commodities or manufactures of both countries, to export *larger* quantities of our own, and import *less* of theirs; so that what is wanting in the value of their merchandise, compared with ours, may be paid in gold and silver. The consequence of which will be, that these metals will be continually increasing with *us*, as far as relates to that particular trade and nation, and decreasing with them. And in what proportion soever their money comes into our country, in that proportion it may truly be affirmed, that our sailors, freighters, merchants, tradesmen, manufacturers, tenants, landlords, duties, taxes, excises, &c. &c. are paid at their expence.

Or, to put the mater in another light; when two countries are exchanging their produce or manufactures with each other, that nation which has the greatest number employed in this reciprocal trade, is said to receive a balance from the other; because the price of the overplus labour must be paid in gold and silver. For example: If there are only ten thousand persons employed in England in making goods or raising some kind of produce for the market of France, and forty thousand in France for the market of England; then we must pay these additional

ditional 30,000 Frenchmen in gold and silver; that is, be at the charge of maintaining them. This is the clearest and justest method of determining the balance between nation and nation: for though a difference in the value of the respective commodities may make some difference in the sum actually paid to balance accounts, yet the general principle, that labour (not money) is the riches of a people, will always prove, that the advantage is on the side of that nation, which has most hands employed in labour.

The *principles* of trade, therefore, being so clear and certain in themselves, and withal so obvious to any man of common capacity and application, it is a very surprising matter how it comes to pass, that both men of good understanding are many times totally ignorant of them, and merchants themselves so divided in their sentiments about them.

As to the first case, perhaps it may be accounted for, if we consider what disadvantageous notions men of a liberal and learned education have imbibed of this noble and interesting science; on which the riches, the strength, the glory, and I may add, the morals and freedom of our country, so essentially depend. Yet it has been represented as a dry unentertaining subject, dark and crabbed, perplexed with endless difficulties, not reducible to any fixed and certain

tain principles; and therefore fit for none, but the mercantile part of the world, to give themselves any trouble concerning it. But upon a fair examination it will perhaps appear, that this representation is very false and injurious.

As to the second, it must be indeed confessed, that merchants themselves are very often divided in their sentiments concerning trade. Sir * Josiah Child, Mr. Gee, Mr. Cary of Bristol, and almost all commercial writers, have long ago taken notice of this difference of opinions. But however strange and

---

* The words of sir Josiah Child strongly corroborate what is here alledged. "Merchants, says he, while
" they are in the busy and eager prosecution of their
" particular trades, although they be very wife and
" good men, are not always the best judges of trade,
" as it relates to the power and profit of a kingdom.
" The reason may be, because their eyes are so continually fixed upon what makes for their peculiar gain
" or loss, that they have no leisure to expatiate or turn
" their thoughts to what is most advantageous to the
" kingdom in general.—
" The like may be said of all shop-keepers, artificers,
" clothiers, and other manufacturers, until they have
" left off their trades, and being rich, become, by the
" purchase of lands, of the same common interest with
" most of their countrymen."
This justly celebrated writer was himself an instance of the truth of this observation. For, if I am not greatly mistaken, he did not write this very treatise, till he had left off trade, and being rich, became, by the purchase of lands, of the same common interest with the rest of his countrymen.

and unaccountable it may appear to persons not conversant in these matters, there is a very strong and convincing reason, when the affair is searched to the bottom, for the disagreeing opinions of different merchants pursuing their respective interests. The leading idea, or the point aimed at by every merchant must be, in the nature of things, and in every country, a balance in favour of himself. But it does not always follow, that this balance is likewise in favour of the nation; much less of other merchants, whose interests may be opposite to his own. While, therefore, each person sees in a favourable light his own branch of commerce, and desires to procure all possible advantages to that traffick, on which the prosperity of himself and his family, perhaps totally, depends, it is but reasonable to expect their sentiments should clash.

Hence therefore some have thought, that a person of a liberal and learned education, not concerned in trade, is better qualified to engage in the study of it, as a *science*, than a merchant himself: because, say they, his mind is freer from the prejudice of self-interest, and therefore more open to conviction in things relating to the general good. They add, that though he may not understand the buying and selling of particular commodities, or the fittest time to bring them to a profitable market, (which is the proper province of a merchant) yet he may understand, in what respects the nature of that trade contributes to the loss or gain of the public, with a degree of evidence, which perhaps the merchant never thought of: as being indeed not concerned, merely as a merchant, in such kinds of disquisitions.

But without pretending to determine who are the best qualified to engage in the study of this most useful and extensive science, let us rather humbly recommend it to the attention of them both. For, undoubtedly, both have their advantages; and perhaps the application of both together, might be more successful than either of them separately. If the one should happen to be less self-interested, by means of his situation in life, and more open to conviction in cases relating to the general good; the other, for the very same reason, is more skilful in the practice of trade, and a better judge, whether the project, perhaps so fair in Theory, is feasible in fact.

As to the private interest of merchants, which is here supposed to be a bias upon their minds, this, most certainly, coincides, for the most part, with the general interest of their country: and so far it can be no argument in their disfavour. But nevertheless, truth obliges us to acknowledge, that in certain cases,* " a merchant may have

---

* " British Merchant," vol. ii. p. 141. 8vo edition, 1721. See likewise the instances there given to confirm this observation.

"a diſtinct intereſt from that of his country. he may thrive by a trade which may prove her ruin." Nay more, he may be impoveriſhed by a trade that is beneficial to her. But undoubtedly, the moment he perceives he is carrying on a loſing trade, he will quit it, and employ his thoughts and his ſubſtance in the proſecution of ſome other. Moreover, as it is a balance in favour of himſelf, which is the principal object of his aims and endeavours, it cannot be expected, but of two trades, both advantageous to the community, he will embrace that which is moſt profitable to himſelf, though it ſhould happen to be leſs gainful to the public. It is a maxim with traders, and a juſtifiable one, to get all that can be got in a legal and honeſt way. And if the laws of their country do give them the permiſſion of carrying on any particular gainful trade, it is their buſineſs, as merchants, to engage in the proſecution of it. As to the great point of national advantage, or diſadvantage, this is properly the concern of others, who ſit at the helm of government, and conſequently whoſe province it is, to frame the laws and regulations relating to trade in ſuch a manner, as may cauſe the private intereſt of the merchant to fall in with the general good of his country.

For theſe reaſons therefore, the appointment of the Board of Trade, muſt certainly
appear

appear a very wife and neceffary inftitution. The intent and defign being, as I humbly conceive, to anfwer this very end. And the honourable members of it may be looked upon, in this light, as the *Guardians of the public welfare*. In prefiding over the general commercial interefts of the kingdom, they are to infpect the feveral branches of traffic that are carried on, and to give notice to the legiflature, whether the profit of the kingdom, or of the merchant, is moft promoted; that the proper remedies, or encouragements may be applied, according as the cafe requires, by ftopping up the former channels of a difadvantageous trade, opening new ones, which may enrich the public and the adventurer together; encouraging him to perfevere, and to enlarge his dealings in every branch, which is beneficial to the community; and, in one word, by enabling the merchant to find his own private advantage in labouring for the good of his country. Self and focial happinefs, in this cafe, muft be made to unite; otherwife it will happen in this, as in moft other affairs, that focial happinefs will not be promoted at all.

And as the affairs of commerce muft, for thefe reafons, ultimately come under the cognizance of the legiflature, it were greatly to be wifhed, that men of eminence and diftinction, whofe birth and fortunes procure them an admiffion into the Britifh fenate,

would

would employ a little more of their time in the cultivation of a science, so worthy of their greatest regard and attention. The interest of their country, and their own, do both concur in requiring such a conduct from them. I beg leave to mention not only the interest of their country, but their own: for it is a most certain fact, though not sufficiently attended to, that the landed gentleman is more deeply concerned in the national effects of an advantageous or disadvantageous commerce, than the merchant himself. If this assertion should appear a paradox to any one, I hope a few lines will convince him of the truth of it.

Suppose then, some general calamity to befal the trade of the kingdom:—Or, to put a more striking case, suppose the mouth of the Thames to be choaked up with sands and marshes, (as that fine river in France, the Rhone, really is) so as to afford no port worth mentioning, for the purposes of commerce: In such a melancholy case, the merchants, manufacturers, owners of ships, sailors, and all the multitudes of tradesmen dependant upon this commerce, would indeed be the first affected, but they would not be the *greatest losers*. For after the first shock, they would easily remove with the best of their effects, and try their fortunes elsewhere. But the landed gentleman, what must he do? he is bound down to the soil, and cannot remove his estate, though the persons are gone, who used to consume the product of it. Thus the evil becomes incurable, and perpetual, with regard to him, and every day encreasing: whereas, with respect to the merchant, it was only a shock at first, which he has the chance of getting the better of, by removing to a more advantageous situation.

It is fervently to be wished, that Providence may never visit us with so terrible a judgment, as the choaking up the mouth of our principal river leading to the metropolis of the kingdom. But the bare supposal of such a case is sufficient to prove, I humbly presume, with irresistible evidence, that the landed gentlemen in the counties adjacent to London, are more deeply interested in the consequences of the trade of London, than the merchants themselves; and, therefore, that those supposed distinctions of landed interest, and trading interest, in the sense they are commonly used, are the most idle and silly, as well as false and injurious, that ever divided mankind.

But above all, we must beg leave to observe, by way of inducement to the landed gentleman, to turn his thoughts to this study, that his very private interest is rather a help, than a detriment to him in the prosecution of it. It puts no wrong bias upon his mind, but directs him to the true point of light, from whence to see, and to judge, of these affairs; which is a circumstance, in some respect, peculiar to his situation.

For, if we suppose the scene still to continue in and about London, (though the same would hold true of any other part of the kingdom) as the private interest of the landed gentlemen arises from the general commerce of the place, he can have no partial views in relation to trade, nor can reap any advantage from monopolies, exclusive companies, or such like destructive artifices. The more persons there are employed in every branch of business, the more there will be to consume the produce of his estate; so that he will have no temptations to complain, that the trade is over-stocked, or wish the promotion of *this* trade, in order to the declension of *that*. In short, his own interest is connected with the good of the whole; so that he cannot but be extremely well qualified to understand, and to promote it, if he will please to make use of the advantages he is happily possessed of.

A BRIEF ESSAY on TRADE.

The Principal ADVANTAGES of FRANCE, with respect to Trade.

I. THE natural produce and commodities of the country.—These are, chiefly, wines, brandies, silk, linen, hemp, and oil. I do not mention corn, for though they raise a great deal, yet, as they are great bread-eaters, they consume a great deal, and have little to spare for exportation. Their harvests also are more precarious than ours, and often fail.

II. The subordination of the common people is an unspeakable advantage to them, in respect to trade. By this means the manufacturers are always kept industrious: they dare not run into shocking lewdness and debauchery; to drunkenness they are not inclined. They * are obliged to enter into the married state; whereby they raise up large families to labour, and keep down the price of it; and, consequently, by working cheaper, enable the merchant to sell the cheaper.

III. The rules and regulations they are obliged to observe in manufacturing their goods, and exposing them to sale, is a great advantage to the credit of their manufactures, and consequently to trade. All sorts of goods for exportation, must undergo an inspection of the proper officer in the public hall: there they are compared with the patterns or samples delivered in before. The bad, and such as do not answer to their samples, are confiscated, with a fine levied upon the offender. By these means, the fraudulent designs of private traders, who would get rich at the public expence, are prevented, and the national manufactory constantly kept up in high credit.

IV. Their excellent roads, their navigable rivers and canals, are of singular advantage to their trade.—Their great roads are always in good order, and always carried on in a strait line, where the nature of the ground will permit; and made at a most

pro-

---

* The law of France obliges all unmarried men to serve as common soldiers in the militia and the army, unless they have particular exceptions, on account of their stations and professions.

prodigious expence; each province being obliged to make and repair their own roads; and yet there is no expence for turnpikes from one end of the kingdom to the other.

Their rivers are indeed, for the moſt part, the work of nature: the Seine, the Loire, the Garonne, and the Rhone, with all the rivers which fall into them, help to carry on a communication with moſt of the great cities of the kingdom.

But their canals are their own proper praiſe; and equally deſerving admiration, on account of their grandeur and contrivance, as for their uſefulneſs to trade, in lowering the price of carriage. Among theſe, that of Languedoc, and the two canals of Orleans and Briare, are worthy to be particularly mentioned. By means of the former, a communication is opened between Bourdeaux and Marſeilles, between the ocean and the Mediterranean, without paſſing through the Straits of Gibraltar, and ſurrounding all the coaſts of Portugal and Spain; and, by virtue of the two latter, an eaſy intercourſe is maintained between all the great towns ſituated on the Seine and the Loire. Many other canals there are, and more ſtill intended to be made, greatly advantageous to their commerce.

V. The French enjoy a great advantage in the goodneſs of their ſugar colonies.—It is not owing to any ſuperior ſkill in them, or wrong

wrong conduct in us, nor yet any greater œconomy in their planters, or profuseness in ours, (for, upon the strictest enquiry, both will be found to be very culpable) that they exceed us in the cheapness and goodness of their commodities; but because our Leeward islands are worn out, being originally of no depth of soil; and the ground is more upon a level, consequently more subject to be burnt up; whereas their islands are still very good. In Martinico particularly, the ground is rich, the soil deep, diversified with high hills, affording copious streams of water, and refreshing shades. Another great advantage which the French have over the English in their sugar colonies, is their Agrarian law, whereby monopolists are prevented from engrossing too much land. So that the number of Whites are greatly encreased, the lands improved, more commodities raised, the planters obliged to a more frugal manner of living, and all things rendered cheaper. By these means Martinico can muster 16,000 fighting men; but Jamaica, which is near three times as large, only 4000. Add to this, that the inhabitants of Old France do not use the tenth part of the sugars for home consumption as the English do; and therefore have that commodity to export again to foreign markets, and with it to encrease the national wealth.

VI. The French colonies receive all their luxuries and refinements of living from their mother

mother-country; which is a very great advantage to it.—They are not suffered, nor indeed doth it appear, that they are much inclined to go to any other shop or market for these things; neither have they set up any manufactures of their own, to the prejudice of their mother-country. Indeed, as to the neceſſaries of life, they ſupply themſelves with them where they can; and frequently buy of the Engliſh. But this is a caſe of neceſſity, which cannot be ſubject to reſtraints. As to articles of luxury, parade, and pleaſure, we very ſeldom hear that they buy any of them from us.

VII. The manner of collecting their duties on ſeveral ſorts of goods imported, is of greater advantage to trade than can eaſily be imagined.—In the port of Bourdeaux (and I take it for granted, ſo good a regulation obtains in other places) there are public warehouſes, very proper and convenient, adjoining to the Cuſtom-houſe. And all proviſions and goods neceſſary for the uſe of their ſugar colonies, are there depoſited by the merchant, 'till the ſhip ſails, duty free, paying only a moderate price for cellarage. When ſhe returns, the ſugars, &c. are landed in the King's warehouſes, where they remain till the importer has found a purchaſer for a proper quantity; then he pays the duty for that, and has it taken away, letting the reſt continue. Or if he intends theſe goods for exportation, there they lie ready and convenient. By this means he is never driven to

ſtraits

straits on account of the King's duty; and is enabled to carry on a very extensive trade with a small stock. The consequence of which is, that many persons are hereby capacitated to enter considerably into commerce, who could not otherwise have done it. For 1000l. sterling in France, will go near as far as 2000l. in England. Not to mention, that as there is no money immediately advanced on account of the King's duty, the whole gains of the merchant will rise only from the money actually in trade: now this is less by near one half to what it would have been, had the duty been all paid at once; consequently he can afford to sell one half less than he must have demanded in the other case.

VIII. Their neighbourhood to Spain, and present connexion with it, is of so great advantage, as to be worth all their trade besides. —For it is certain, they get more from the Spaniards than all the trading nations in Europe. Their poor from Perigord, Limosin, and other places, come yearly into Spain to reap their corn, and gather in their vintage; and carry back what they have earned to spend in France. The fishermen from Bayonne, and the neighbouring places, supply them with great quantities both of fresh and salt fish, to eat on fast-days, and to keep Lent. The pedlars and shop-keepers in Spain, are most French, who retire into their own country when they have made their fortunes. The towns in Languedoc supply them with cloth, silks, and stockings; Rouen with
hats.

hats, and coarse linen stuffs; Abbeville, with superfine cloths; Amiens and Arras, with worsted and camblet stuffs; and Lions, with all sorts of rich silks, gold and silver lace, &c. for their consumption both in Europe and America. In short, the greatest part of the produce of the mines of Potosi is brought into France. Hence it is that their payments are all in silver; and gold is more scarce in France, in the currency of coin, than silver is in England. A plain proof, that they have the great trade to Spain, as we have to Portugal.

IX. Their address in drawing raw materials from other countries to work up in their own, serves greatly to enlarge and extend their trade. France produces some wool and silk; but not a fourth part of what they manufacture. Wool they import from Barbary, the Levant, and Spain. They also bring wool from Switzerland. Some little perhaps is run from England; but, I have good reason to believe, not much. The quantity from Ireland is very considerable; which is owing to our own wrong policy. The best of their raw silk they draw from Piemont, the Levant, Italy, and Spain. Their cotton is brought from the Levant, and from their sugar colonies. And the ashes for making soap, at Marseilles, are chiefly imported from Egypt.

X. They reap unspeakable advantage, by the permission and encouragement given to foreign

foreign merchants and manufacturers to settle among them.—By this good policy the price of labour is always kept sufficiently low. A competition and emulation are raised, who shall work, and sell the cheapest; which must turn out greatly to the national advantage, though it may not be so favourable to the private interest of individuals. For these reasons, the government is particularly gentle and indulgent to foreigners. And the situation of the country is greatly assistant to this disposition of the government.—France is surrounded with populous, that is prolific nations, who have no trade and manufactures of their own to employ their poor. Flanders, all Germany on the side of the Rhine, Switzerland, Savoy, and some parts of Italy, pour their supernumerary hands every year into France; where they are caressed, and received into the army, or the manufacture, according to their inclinations. The Rhone is so easy and cheap a conveyance, for the swarms of inhabitants bordering on the lake of Geneva, that so small a sum as one shilling, or eighteen pence each person, will bring them to the chief manufacturing town in the kingdom, viz. Lions. And there are said to be no less than ten thousand Swiss and Germans employed in that city. The numbers also in all the other commercial towns are very great, and daily increasing.

XI. The English monopolies, which are so
destruc-

destructive to the interests of Great Britain, become, for the very same reason, of the greatest benefit and advantage to France.—Marseilles is a flagrant, and a melancholy proof of this assertion: For the trade of this place hath flourished and increased just in the same proportion, as that of our Turky company sunk and declined. All the fine streets and new buildings of the city, date their original from this period. So that we may truly say, they were built, and are now supported, by the exclusive Turky company of England. Moreover, the English Hudson's-Bay company is the only cause, which can make the French settlements in so wretched a country as the northern parts of Canada, to flourish; with so difficult and dangerous a navigation, as that up the bay of St. Lawrence. It is this, and no other, is the cause that enables them to extend their colonies, and to undersell the English in all the articles of furr; which they apparently do in times of peace.

XII. The publick stock of wealth is greatly increased, by foreigners of all countries travelling among them.—The advantages from hence accruing have not been so much attended to, as, I humbly think, they justly deserve. For while these foreigners reside in the country, they not only pay for their food and board at an high rate, but they also cloath themselves with the manufactures of it, and buy many curiofities. But this is not all: for having contracted a liking to the produce and manufactures of the country they traveled in, they continue to ufe them when they are returned to their own; and fo introduce them to the knowledge, efteem, and approbation of others: this begets a demand; and a demand for them draws on a correfpondence, and a fettled commerce. Thefe are the advantages which the French enjoy by fuch numbers of foreigners travelling among them; whereas they fcarce ever travel themfelves; and by that means circulate the money in their own country.

XIII. France enjoys no fmall advantage, as it doth not lofe much by the article of fmuggling, in comparifon to what England doth.—This is owing to the ftrictnefs of their government, the many fpies they have upon every man's actions, and being able to punifh the flighteft offence more feverely, and in a more fummary way than we can, or is confiftent with a free conftitution to do.

The Principal DISADVANTAGES *of* Trade *with regard to* FRANCE.

I. THE firſt diſadvantage to a free trade is the government, which is arbitrary and deſpotic; and therefore ſuch as a merchant would not chuſe to live under, if he knows the ſweets of liberty in another country, and has no attachment of family, or intereſt to keep him ſtill in France.—It muſt be acknowledged, his property, generally ſpeaking, is ſecure enough; but his perſon is not ſo. To explain this, we muſt beg leave to obſerve, that though there are fixed and ſtated laws in France to decide all caſes of property, and criminal cauſes, as here in England; ſo that a man may know the rules he is to be governed by in thoſe reſpects, and can have an open trial for his life and fortune; yet there are no laws to aſcertain the nature of political offences, or to circumſcribe the power of the judge: ſo that he muſt be intirely at the mercy of the Lieutenant de Police, and his deputies; who can impriſon him at will, without aſſigning any reaſon, or bringing any evidence to confront him. And therefore his only

only security consists, in being continually lavish in the praise of the king and the ministry, and in saying nothing which may afford the least pretence to the spies, who swarm all over the kingdom, to inform against him.

II. The second disadvantage to the freedom of trade, is the Romish religion; which has added to its many other absurdities, a spirit of cruelty and persecution, so repugnant to the scope and tendency of the gospel.—Therefore a protestant merchant, if at the same time a conscientious man, will find himself very often reduced to great difficulties, in order to avoid, on the one hand, the sin of hypocrisy, by compliances against his conscience, or, on the other, the danger attending the exercise of his religion, and the educating of his children in the protestant way. This, I say, will often happen, even at present; though the bigotry of the court of France is not near so great as it was in former times.

III. Another great burden, and consequently a disadvantage to the trade of France, is, the great number of religious of both sexes.—The lowest computation of these amounts to near three hundred thousand persons: a great part of which number might, and would be employed in trade and manufactures; and the rest might be useful to society in other spheres. But that is not all; they are a very heavy weight upon

upon the public. Vast estates are appropriated for the support of some of these religious orders, whose fund is continually accumulating, not only by legacies and donations, but also by whatever fortune each person is possessed of, at the time of taking the vow. And others, who are of the Mendicant orders, and are allowed to have no property, become a continual tax upon the industry and charity of the people; and these mostly of the middling and lower sort. Not to mention the increasing riches and dead wealth in all their churches.

IV. A fourth great disadvantage to the trade of France, is their numerous and poor nobility.—The nature and constitution of that government require the notion of birth and family to be kept up very high, as it will always create an indigent nobility, and consequently dependant upon the court for such preferments as may not deroge, or bring a stain upon their family. Moreover, the same refined policy induces the court to make the military service be esteemed the most honourable; as it must render the whole body of the nobility soldiers to fight their battles; the richer serving for glory, and the poorer for an honourable support. The consequence of all this is, that they heartily despise the Bourgeois§, that is, the merchant and tradesman:

§ In France the inhabitants are usually distinguished by three ranks, or orders; the noblesse, the bourgeois,

man: and he, when he gets rich, is as desirous of quitting so dishonourable an employ, wherein his riches cannot secure him from insult and contempt. Being therefore ambitious of raising his own family to be of the Noblesse, he leaves off trade as soon as he can, and breeds up his sons to the military profession, or purchases some office in the law or civil government, which may ennoble them.

V. The trade of France suffers another inconveniency by the nature of its taxes.— Some of these, in certain provinces, are very arbitrary; as the Taille, which is levied mostly

and the paisans. Each of these are totally distinct from the other. The posterity of the noblesse are all noblesse, though ever so poor, and though not honoured with the titles of Count, Marquis, &c. as noblemen are here in England. The posterity of a bourgeois, though ever so rich, and though the family have left off trade a hundred years ago, are still but bourgeois, until they are ennobled by patent, or have wiped off the disgrace of having been merchants, by some signal military service, or have purchased some honourable employ. Therefore when the noblesse call the merchants, bourgeois, (burgesses) they mean it as a term of infamy and reproach, answering to that of, pitiful low mechanic, in English. Indeed, by some ordinances, the noblesse are permitted to engage in certain branches of foreign and wholesale trade, without bringing any stain upon their family. But these permissions will have very little efficacy to induce the nobility to turn merchants, as long as the military service is so highly exalted in credit and reputation above merchandize. The very genius of the government makes it a scandal not to be a soldier: Laws will have little force against this.

mostly upon the poor peasants and manufacturers in the country villages. Others are very heavy; as the duty upon salt, which is shockingly oppressive. Others again, though not quite so oppressive, are yet equally improperly laid, because they are upon the necessaries of life, which are to feed the tradesman, and to victual the shipping. Thus, for example, all sorts of provisions, corn, wine, butchers meat, poultry, eggs, fish, garden-stuff, and fruit, pay a duty at the entrance of some of their great cities. There are duties also lately laid upon soap and candles. And in the Païs des Etats, where the most grievous of these imposts are not levied, they lay a provincial duty upon all things going in or out of that province; which makes the merchandize so passing through, become the dearer at a foreign market.

VI. The maitrises, which so generally prevail in France, is a clog to the trade of the country.—These maitrises are much the same as our companies in towns corporate; only we have this advantage, that in England their pernicious effects can be more easily eluded by having shops, &c. within glass windows. Besides, our best manufacturing towns, such as Birmingham, Manchester, Leeds, and even four-fifths of London itself, viz. Westminster, Southwark, and all the suburbs, have no companies at all.

all. Whereas, in France, all tradesmen are obliged to be free of their proper maitrise, before they can set up. The fine for this, in some trades, is very considerable. And there is also, in time of war, an annual demand of a certain proportion of men out of each maitrise; which is understood to imply a sum of money by way of equivalent. Thus, the more these maitrises become useful to supply the exigencies of the government at a pinch, the more privileges they will acquire; and the greater the privilege is of any particular company, the less will be the general trade of the country.

VII. The French sustain some disadvantage by their monopolies and exclusive charters.—They have an East-India Company at Port l'Orient: Marseilles is a free port for the Levant and Barbary trade; whereas there is a duty of 20 *per cent.* upon all merchandize of those countries, if imported into any other port of France in the Mediterranean. And even at Marseilles, there is a particular exclusive company for importing corn and wool from Africa. Lions is free for all silk entering, or going out; whereas there is an heavy duty in the neighbouring towns; by which means, Lions may be said to have an exclusive charter. And there is good reason to conclude, there is something of the same nature for the Turky cloth at Carcassonne, the silk and worsted stockings at Nismes, the cloathing

cloathing for the foldiery at Lodeve, the fuperfine cloth at Abbeville, the stuffs at Amiens, the camblets at Arras, the painted linens and cottons at Rouen, &c.

VIII. The French labour under no small difadvantage on account of the expence they are at in the article of shipping.—They have more men to navigate their ships than the English, because they are not so expert sailors. They must carry some supernumerary landsmen, by the King's orders: they must have many officers to govern these men, because the merchant is to be refponfible for them when the ship returns. These officers will have a grand table, a cook, and new bread every day. The ship lies long in port, if sent to the West-Indies to difpofe of the cargo: because their Creolians are said to be so dishonest, that they do not care to trust them with commiffions; and so the expences of the officers and of the crew run very high. Add to this, that the officer belonging to the marine in France, will find ways and means to give great trouble to the merchant, both as to the choice of sailors, and of officers, unless he is properly confidered: which is generally done by buying some ship stores of himself, or friends, at an exorbitant price.

IX. The two national vices of the French, gaming and fine clothes, is a great hurt to their trade.—These expences cannot be fupported

ported but by a large profit; and that will always leſſen the demand at a foreign market, if their neighbours can afford to ſell cheaper. Not to mention the ſwift ruin which gaming ſometimes brings on, and the loſs of time occaſioned by it.

X. The ſituation of the French ports, are a great diſadvantage to them, with reſpect to the Hamburg and northern trade: and in regard to the ſouthern and Weſt-Indies, they are not better ſituated; and are not near ſo many, nor ſo good as ours, eſpecially if we take Ireland into the account. They have only an advantage with reſpect to the Mediterranean.

XI. The farming of the revenue is another great diſadvantage to the commerce of France. For theſe Farmers have moſt immoderate profits, and live in all the ſplendor and expence of the firſt Princes of the blood. And as they act by the King's authority, they tyranniſe over the ſubjects with impunity.— Yet I cannot ſee how the French government can be without ſuch a ſet of people. For when money is wanted, they are ready to lend, while the ſubject is afraid: therefore they borrow of the ſubject, giving their own ſecurities, and then lend to the government at an advanced price, paying themſelves, as the duties are collected.

To theſe diſadvantages, it has been intimated, I ought to have mentioned their

many

many holidays, on which they muſt not work, and their pompous proceſſions, which draw the people a gazing after them.—The thought did occur to me before, at the time of writing the firſt edition: but I ſuppreſſed it then, and now beg leave to aſſign the reaſons; viz. In the firſt place, theſe things are greatly wearing off in France every day; ſo that the loſs of time is not ſo conſiderable, as one may imagine. Secondly, Allowing that ſome time is idled away during theſe holidays, and in ſeeing proceſſions, &c. ſtill, if we caſt up the account of the time and money which are ſpent here in England by all ſorts of manufacturers, in horſe-races, cock-fightings, cricket-matches, bull-baitings, but more eſpecially in mobbing and electioneering, (all which are not in France) I am perſuaded, we ſhall find the advantage gained over them, on the ſcore of their holidays and proceſſions, to be none at all; and that upon comparing both articles together, the amount of the diſadvantages will be found to be greater on our ſide, than on theirs.

The principal ADVANTAGES *of* GREAT BRITAIN *with respect to Trade.*

I. THE natural produce and commodities of the country; corn, wool, lead, tin, copper, coal, butter, cheese, tallow, leather.—All which are not to be found in France, in that plenty and abundance they are in England.

II. The number, goodness, and situation of our ports.—Those on the western side of Great-Britain (especially if we reckon Ireland a part of ourselves, and include both islands under *one general interest,* as in reason and policy we ought to do) are almost as well situated for the southern trade, as the French: they are four times as many in number, and much better for safety, and depth of water. And as to the North and Baltic trade, the French can come into no comparison with ours.

III. Nature has been very bountiful, in bestowing on us such excellent fisheries; particularly the herring-fishery, on the northern coasts of Scotland, and the cod on the south-west of Ireland.—These great advantages are always in our power to cultivate and improve; and it is our fault, and our reproach, that we do not.

IV. England enjoys another advantage by means of its free government.—A merchant can go to law with the crown, as eafily as with a private fubject. The judges are for the life of the prince on the throne, and confequently not under the immediate influence of the court. No man's perfon can be detained, but a reafon muft be given, and the matter brought to an open trial, where his equals are to be his judges, and to decide between him and the crown, whether he hath committed an offence againft the ftate, or not.

V. Another ineftimable blefling, and a great advantage, confidered merely in a commercial view, is the liberty of confcience we enjoy in thefe kingdoms.—Every man is permitted to worfhip God in the way he thinks the right and true, without fear or referve; and may educate his children in his own religion. The Roman catholics, indeed, are under fome legal difcouragements: but it is plain, the legiflature confidered them rather as a political, than a religious fect, when thofe laws were enacted. And the prefent government, by its conduct towards them, has given them fufficiently to underftand, that they fhall not be difturbed in the free exercife of their religion, provided they will give no difturbance to the ftate in civil affairs,

affairs, by siding with its enemies. This, surely, is but a reasonable demand: and here the matter seems to rest.

VI. England has always enjoyed an advantage in trade, as its manufacturers have ever been in high repute for their skill and ingenuity.—Our locks, chains, clock-work, mathematical instruments, and all sorts of cutlery ware, far exceed all others at this day, and are deservedly preferred by foreign nations. And our sailors are considerably superior to the French, in their art and dexterity.

VII. England enjoys a very visible advantage over France, as the whole bulk of our people may be concerned in trade, if they please, without any disreputation to their families.—The profession of a merchant is esteemed full as honourable as that of an officer. And no man need leave off trade, when he finds himself rich, in order to be respected as a gentleman. It is likewise no scandal for younger brothers of the most antient families to be bred up to trade and business.

VIII. The island of Jamaica has some advantages over any of the French islands, on account of its situation, to carry on a beneficial trade with the Spanish Main; the sweets of which have been so sufficiently felt during the late war, as to need no further illustration.

tion. And this island is capable of great improvements in many other respects.

IX. The very wants of Great-Britain, in one respect, might be turned into a singular advantage over the French in another.—It is certain, France cannot carry on a trade to most countries with that advantage to the country it trades with, as the English can.—For example: the English can trade with the Spaniards to *mutual* advantage: if the English export cloth and stuffs to Spain, they can take off fruits, oil, and wine, by way of barter. Whereas the French can make no use of these commodities, having so much of their own growth both to use, and to spare.—A consideration of this nature, well timed, and strongly urged, might have a good effect upon the Spanish court, to induce them to favour the English commerce, and discountenance the French. It is owing to the successful application of Sir Paul Methuen on this very head, when Envoy to the court of Portugal, that the English at this day enjoy the whole trade of Portugal, and that the French, in a manner, are excluded.

X. The low interest of money, and the easy and expeditious transfers in the funds, give to Great-Britain a manifest advantage in the affairs of commerce. For were the interest as high as in France, the exportation of our manufactures would be much dearer, as every exporter would expect to get a profit superior to the interest of money; the sure consequence of which would be, a lessening of the quantity exported.—Besides, the merchants of London, by means of East-India bonds, and the quick transfers of stocks, are enabled to make a profit of their money, when not employed in trade; by which means they can afford to buy and sell for less gains.

The principal DISADVANTAGES *of* Great-Britain *with regard to Trade.*

I. THE first and *capital* disadvantage, is the want of subordination in the lower class of people.—This is attended with dreadful consequences, both in a commercial and a moral view. If they are subject to little or no control, they will run into vice: vice is attended with expence, which must be supported either by an high price for their labour, or by methods still more destructive. The end of all is poverty and disease; and so they become a loathsome burden to the public. Nothing is more visible, than the great difference between the morals and industry of the manufacturing poor in France, and in England. In the former, they are

sober,

sober, frugal, and laborious: they marry, and have flocks of children, whom they bring up to labour. In the latter, they are given up to drunkenness and debauchery: the streets swarm with prostitutes, who spread the infection, till they are carried to an hospital, or their grave. The men are as bad as can be described; who become more vicious, more indigent and idle, in proportion to the advance of wages, and the cheapness of provisions: great numbers of both sexes never working at all, while they have any thing to spend upon their vices.

II. The prodigious expence of electioneering, is another fatal stab to trade and industry.—It is not only so much money spent, but it is spent mostly upon manufacturers; and so it gives them a taste for idleness, and brings on an habit of drunkenness, and extravagance. The want also of subordination, just now complained of, is mostly to be imputed to the same cause, as it sets them above control, frees them from all restraint, and brings down the rich to pay their court to them, contrary to the just and proper order of society.

III. Another very great burden on the English commerce, is the vast numbers of poor; and those every day increasing.—If we trace the matter to its fountain-head, we shall find it to be owing principally to the same causes.

causes, viz. electioneering, and the want of subordination. And, if a calculation was made of the expences of electioneering, and the ruinous consequences of it, together with the annual poor-tax, I am very sure it would exceed, in the proportion, what France expends in maintaining three hundred thousand religious of both sexes: so that we gain no advantage over France in this respect, through our own dissoluteness and ill management.

IV. Our trade is greatly burthened by the nature of most of our taxes, and the manner of collecting them.—The customs on the goods imported, make those goods come much dearer to the consumer, than they would do, if the consumer himself was to pay the duty: and this becomes a strong temptation to our people to smuggle. The taxes upon the necessaries of life, are in fact so many taxes upon trade and industry: and such must be accounted the duties upon soap, coal, candles, salt, and leather. Likewise the duties upon the importation of foreign raw materials, to be employed in our own manufactures, are so many fetters and chains to prevent the progress of labour, and circulation of wealth. These imposts were first laid on, under a notion of promoting the landed interest; but happy would it have been for these kingdoms, if the landed gentlemen

tlemen had underſtood their intereſt, before they attempted to ſhew their zeal in promoting it.

Moreover, the expenſive manner of collecting all our cuſtoms, is ſtill an additional diſadvantage; ſuch as the multiplication and ſplitting of offices, patent-places, fees, ſinecures, penſions, &c. &c. Theſe things, indeed, create a dependance upon the court, and are ſaid to ſtrengthen the hands of the government; but if they do ſo in one reſpect, they weaken it much more in another. They give too juſt cauſe for complaint; the beſt friends of the preſent eſtabliſhment are grieved to ſee any meaſures which they cannot vindicate. Repeated murmurs, where there is a real foundation for them, naturally tend to alienate the affections of the bulk of the people, which above all things ſhould be guarded againſt; becauſe in times of actual danger, it is the people, and not place-men and penſioners, who can ſave the government, and oppoſe themſelves againſt the invaſions of foreign, or the inſurrections of domeſtic, enemies: as was plainly ſeen in the caſe of the late rebellion.

V. The great number of ſmugglers in England, are of infinite detriment to trade. —They carry nothing but bullion, or wool, out of the kingdom, and return moſtly with the commodities of France. They are the necessary cause of creating many offices, maintaining sloops, smacks, &c. to guard against them; and they furnish a pretence for adding many more. Thus they become doubly mischievous. They tempt others to do the like, for fear of being ruined in their lawful trades by being undersold. The practice of smuggling debauches the morals of the common people, it leads them into perjury, and tutors them up in all vice and extravagance. So many expences incurred, so many deficiencies in the revenue, must be made np some other way; that is, by duties not so liable to be embezzled. And, therefore, fact it is, that every man, in paying taxes for land, &c. pays for the damage done, or caused by smuggling. And yet, 'till there is a proper subordination introduced, and the qualification for voting something altered from what is at present, it is easy to see, there never can be any effectual cure for this growing evil. Smugglers are, for the most part, inhabitants of boroughs and towns corporate: they, or their relations friends, dealers, acquaintances, &c. are *voters*; and—*Verbum sat sapienti.*

VI. Our monopolies, public companies, and corporate charters, are the bane and destruction of a free trade.—By the charter of the East-India company, at least nine thousand nine hundred and ninety-nine British subjects,

subjects, out of ten thousand, without having committed any fault to deserve such a punishment, are excluded from trading any where beyond the Cape of Good Hope. By the charter of the Turky company, a like, or a greater number, are excluded from having any commerce with the whole Turkish empire. The Hudson's Bay company engrosses all the furr trade with the Indians, in an extent of country almost as large as half Europe. Thus the interest of nine thousand nine hundred and ninety-nine fellow-subjects, is sacrificed, in so many respects, for the sake of a single one. The whole nation suffers in its commerce, and is debarred trading to more than three-fourths of the globe to enrich a few rapacious directors. They get wealthy the very same way by which the public becomes poor, viz. first, by exporting small quantities of our own manufactures, in order to have an exorbitant profit; and, 2dly, by importing but a few of the raw materials of foreign countries, that they may have the higher price for what they bring home.—A double mischief! equally fatal to the community, both by the smallness of their exports and imports.

And as to corporate charters, and companies of trades, they are likewise so many monopolies in the places to which they belong, to the great detriment of national commerce.—

To convince any one of this, let him but suppose a set of town and country butchers frequenting the same market; and that the country butchers were excluded for a market or two; would not the town butchers raise their price? *i. e.* put all their fellow-citizens under contribution, by means of this privilege? And doth not every other company the same in all things they sell? And what is the consequence?—A general dearness among one another, which must light at last upon the foreign trade, and therefore diminish the quantity to be exported.

VII. Our imprudence and narrow-spiritedness in not inviting foreigners to settle among us, is another material disadvantage to the English trade.—Foreigners can never get rich in a strange country, but by working cheaper or better than the natives. And if they do so, though individuals may suffer, the public is certainly a gainer; as there is so much merchandize to be exported upon cheaper terms, or so much saved to the merchant, whereby he may afford to export the cheaper. Not to mention, that by this means the price of labour is continually beat down, combinations of journeymen against their masters are prevented, industry is encouraged, and an emulation excited. All which are greatly for the public good.

Besides, a foreigner just escaped from slavery

slavery and oppression, when he gets rich in a land of liberty and plenty, is not likely to return home, but will settle among us, and become one of ourselves, with his whole family. And what are *all* Englishmen but the descendants of foreigners? In short, it is the same weak policy to prevent foreigners settling among us, as it is in the poor about London, to oppose the Welsh and Irish coming up to work in the gardens, and carry in the harvest; not considering, that if the gardener or farmer cannot have his work done cheap, he cannot afford to sell the garden-stuff, bread, &c. cheap to them. So that they themselves find their account in the cheapness of the labour of these persons. Indeed, the English should give *more* encouragement, if possible, to strangers than France doth; as for many other reasons, so particularly for this, that the Flemish, Germans, Swiss, Piedmontise, Italians, &c. can arrive at most of the manufacturing towns in France at a trifling expence; whereas the long journey from their own country, and the passage over into England, are a very great discouragement to foreign manufacturers to come to settle here.

VIII. Our ill-judged policy, and unnatural jealousy, in cramping the commerce and manufactures of *Ireland*, is another very great bar against extending our trade.—This
is

is a most unaccountable infatuation, which has not the shadow of a public and national reason to defend it. For if Ireland gets rich, what is the consequence? England will be rich too, and France will be the poorer. The wool which is now smuggled from* Ireland into France, and manufactured there, and from thence sent to oppose our own commodities at foreign markets, would be manufactured in Ireland; the French would lose the benefit of it, the Irish would get it:—the rents of the estates in Ireland would rise; and then the money would soon find its way into England. Besides, the Irish might be incorporated into the English parliament, and make one nation with ourselves, bearing an equal share of taxes, and so easing England, at the same time that Ireland is enriched.—But more of this hereafter.

IX. Want of a less expensive way of repairing our roads; want of more navigable rivers

---

* A clergyman, whose living is in the west of Ireland, assured me, that just after the peace, the wool smugglers of his parish got upwards of 50 per cent. by the wool they sold to the French.—As long as this is the case, laws and restrictions will signify nothing. If we have a mind to prevent the Irish sending their wool to France, we must make it their *interest* to keep it at home; which can never be done, but by permitting them to manufacture it themselves, and export it to any market they can.

rivers and canals; are a very great difadvantage to England, in comparifon to France.—Every one muft be fenfible of the heavy tax, which fo many turnpikes lay upon trade; and how bad even the turnpike roads are in many parts of the country, diftant from London. We have no canals to open a communication between city and city, river and river, though our country is much better adapted for them than France.

X. We labour under a very great difadvantage, as moft of our leeward iflands are now worn out, and indeed were never fo fertile, or fo lafting a foil as the French; therefore they require a greater expence to cultivate them: fo that our fugars muft come the dearer to Europe. Befides, as we ufe fo much for home confumption, we have the lefs to fpare for foreign markets. But the greateft misfortune is, that the planters in thefe fmall iflands are fuffered to monopolize as much land as they pleafe; by which means the plantations are engroffed in a few hands, and the number of whites is daily decreafing; fo that the fugar colonies now confume much lefs of the produce of the mother country; and yet, in time of danger, England is obliged to be at the expence of a greater force to protect them, as they are lefs able to defend themfelves.

XI. England labours under a peculiar difadvantage

advantage in comparison to France, as its colonies are not so much under the command of their mother country, nor so studious of her welfare.—In many of these colonies several manufactures are set up, and more intended to be erected, which will greatly interfere with the trade of England. And we must expect that this evil will not decrease, but increase by time, unless an effectual method can speedily be put in practice, to divert the thoughts of our colonists from these pursuits, to some others, equally serviceable to them, and less detrimental to us. Besides, they not only set up manufactures of their own in opposition to ours, but they purchase those luxuries and refinements of living from foreigners, which we could furnish them with. It is computed, that they are supplied with at least one third of these articles from foreign nations; amongst whom the French come in for the greatest share.

XII. We also suffer a further inconvenience in not inviting foreigners to travel into England, and spend their money among us; and in being too fond of travelling ourselves.—It is certain, England has as many curiosities for a foreigner to observe, as any country in the world: the whole island, and every thing belonging to it, being in many respects different from the Continent, and worthy the

the attention of a stranger. And even as to fine paintings, original statutes, and antiques, we have prodigious collections of them in private hands, though little known even to our own countrymen, for want of a public and general catalogue. Moreover, our English travellers in France and Italy, are continually making new collections in order to carry home, and embellish their own country. And yet, our gentry are so shy to strangers, the servants expect so much vails, and the common people are so rude and affronting, that very few care to travel in such a country.

XIII. The high price of labour is another insuperable bar to a large trade.—The causes of which are such as have been assigned already, viz. electioneering; the corrupt morals of the people; taxes on the necessaries of life; monopolies, public companies, and corporate charters of trades.

XIV. We suffer a very great detriment through the want of public inspectors, to see that our manufactures produce every thing good in its kind; that they give good weight and measure, and fold the worst side outermost. And what is still worse, where such have been appointed, they have degenerated, through some unhappy abuse, so far as to increase the evil they were intended to correct.

XV. Add to all these, the discouragements and oppositions which the most generous scheme will too often meet with from self-interested and designing men, who pervert the invaluable blessing of liberty, and a free constitution, to some of the worst of purposes. In a despotic kingdom, the ministry have none to oppose them in their good designs: but among us, let their plan be ever so well calculated for the public good, yet if it clashes with the private interest of any particular persons, trading companies, or boroughs, (as it necessarily must do) then it is opposed, under various pretences, by the united force of false patriots, who inflame the populace with words and names, and blacken and misrepresent the best designs in the most malevolent manner.

Besides, in an absolute government, there is no possibility of gaining preferment by making one's self formidable to the ministry. Whereas in England, it is the sure road to it. A bold plausible speaker in the House, embarrasses the schemes of the ministry, not because he thinks them wrong, but because he expects to be *bought off* by a place, or a pension. A news-writer, or a pamphleteer, puts every measure of the court in the most odious light, in order to make his paper sell the better, or to be thought considerable enough to be retained on their side.

On the other hand, the ministry are too apt

apt to endeavour to quash a motion, not because it was a bad one, but because it came from the party in the opposition. A good motion, a public-spirited and generous proposal, would raise the credit of the authors of them too high with the people, were they carried into execution, to the detriment of the ministry. Therefore, *salus* sui, not *salus* populi, *suprema lex esto*.

Thus it is on both sides: and an honest, well-meaning person, whose views are single, and who is conscious to himself of no other attachment but the good of his country, cannot but lament these pernicious evils. And the more so, as he must despair of seeing them effectually removed or cured, without introducing worse evils in their stead; unless men were much honester, and more upright than they are; which, it is to be feared, is not likely to be soon the case.

THREE ESSAYS.

I. On the BALANCE of TRADE.
II. On the JEALOUSY of TRADE.
III. On the BALANCE of POWER.

By DAVID HUME, Esq.

ESSAY I.

On the BALANCE of TRADE.

IT is very usual, in nations ignorant of the nature of commerce, to prohibit the exportation of commodities, and to preserve among themselves whatever they think valuable and useful. They do not consider, that, in this prohibition, they act directly contrary to their intention; and that the more is exported of any commodity, the more will be raised at home, of which they themselves will always have the first offer.

It is well known to the learned, that the ancient laws of Athens rendered the exportation

tation of figs criminal; that being supposed a species of fruit so excellent in Attica, that the Athenians deemed it too delicious for the palate of any foreigner. And in this ridiculous prohibition they were so much in earnest, that informers were thence called *sycophants* among them, from two Greek words, which signify figs and discoverer‡. There are proofs in many old acts of parliament, of the same ignorance in the nature of commerce, particularly in the reign of Edward III. And to this day, in France, the exportation of corn is almost always prohibited; in order, as they say, to prevent famines; though it is evident, that nothing contributes more to the frequent famines, which so much distress that fertile country.

The same jealous fear, with regard to money, has also prevailed among several nations; and it required both reason and experience to convince any people, that these prohibitions serve to no other purpose than to raise the exchange against them, and produce a still greater exportation.

These errors, one may say, are gross and palpable: But there still prevails, even in nations well acquainted with commerce, a strong jealousy with regard to the balance of trade, and a fear, that all their gold and silver may be leaving them. This seems to me, almost in every case, a groundless apprehension; and I should as soon dread, that all our springs and rivers should be exhausted,

as

‡ Plut. De Curiositate.

as that money should abandon a kingdom where there are people and industry. Let us carefully preserve these latter advantages; and we need never be apprehensive of losing the former.

It is easy to observe, that all calculations concerning the balance of trade, are founded on very uncertain facts and suppositions. The custom-house books are allowed to be an insufficient ground of reasoning; nor is the rate of exchange much better; unless we consider it with all nations, and know also the proportions of the several sums remitted; which one may safely pronounce impossible. Every man, who has ever reasoned on this subject, has always proved his theory, whatever it was, by facts and calculations, and by an enumeration of all the commodities sent to all foreign kingdoms.

The writings of Mr. Gee struck the nation with an universal panic, when they saw it plainly demonstrated, by a detail of particulars, that the balance was against them for so considerable a sum as must leave them without a single shilling in five or six years. But luckily, twenty years have since elapsed with an expensive foreign war, yet is it commonly supposed, that money is still more plentiful among us than in any former period.

Nothing can be more entertaining on this head than Dr. Swift; an author so quick in discerning the mistakes and absurdities of others. He says, in his " Short View of the

the State of Ireland," that the whole cash of that kingdom formerly amounted but to 500,000l. that out of this the Irish remitted every year a neat million to England, and had scarcely any other source from which they could compensate themselves, and little other foreign trade than the importation of French wines, for which they paid ready money. The consequence of this situation, which must be owned to be disadvantageous, was, that, in a course of three years, the current money of Ireland, from 500,000l. was reduced to less than two. And at present, I suppose, in a course of 30 years, it is absolutely nothing. Yet I know not how, that opinion of the advance of riches in Ireland, *which gave the Doctor so much indignation, seems still to continue and gain ground with every body.*

In short, this apprehension of the wrong balance of trade, appears of such a nature, that it discovers itself, wherever one is out of humour with the ministry, or is in low spirits; and as it can never be refuted by a particular detail of all the exports, which counterbalance the imports, it may here be proper to form a general argument, that may prove the impossibility of this event, as long as we preserve our people, and our industry.

Suppose four-fifths of all the money in Britain to be annihilated in one night, and the nation reduced to the same condition, with regard to specie, as in the reigns of the

I I   Harrys

Harrys and Edwards, what would be the consequence? Must not the price of all labour and commodities sink in proportion, and every thing be sold as cheap as they were in those ages? What nation could then dispute with us in any foreign market, or pretend to navigate or to sell manufactures at the same price, which to us would afford sufficient profit? In how little time, therefore, must this bring back the money which we had lost, and raise us to the level of all the neighbouring nations? Where, after we have arrived, we immediately lose the advantage of the cheapness of labour and commodities; and the farther flowing in of money is stopped by our fulness and repletion.

Again, suppose, that all the money of Britain were multiplied fivefold in a night, must not the contrary effect follow? Must not all labour and commodities rise to such an exorbitant height, that no neighbouring nations could afford to buy from us; while, their commodities, on the other hand, became comparatively so cheap, that, in spite of all the laws which could be formed, they would be run in upon us, and our money flow out; till we fall to a level with foreigners, and lose that great superiority of riches, which hath laid us under such disadvantages?

Now, it is evident, that the same causes, which would correct these exorbitant inequalities,

qualities, were they to happen miraculously, must prevent their happening in the common course of nature, and must for ever, in all neighbouring nations, preserve money nearly proportionable to the art and industry of each nation. All water, wherever it communicates, remains always at a level. Ask naturalists the reason; they tell you, that, were it to be raised in any one place, the superior gravity of that part not being balanced, must depress it, till it meet a counterpoise; and that the same cause, which redresses the inequality when it happens, must for ever prevent it, without some violent external operation.*

Can one imagine, that it had ever been possible, by any laws, or even by any art or industry, to have kept all the money in Spain, which the galleons have brought from the Indies? Or that all commodities could be sold in France for a tenth of the price which they would yield on the other side of the Pyrenees, without finding their way thither, and draining from that immense treasure?

---

* There is another cause, though more limited in its operation, which checks the wrong balance of trade, to every particular nation to which the kingdom trades. When we import more goods than we export, the exchange turns against us, and this becomes a new encouragement to export; as much as the charge of carriage and insurance of the money which becomes due would amount to. For the exchange can never rise higher than that sum.

treasure? What other reason, indeed, is there, why all nations, at present, gain in their trade with Spain and Portugal; but because it is impossible to heap up money, more than any fluid, beyond its proper level? The sovereigns of these countries have shown, that they wanted not inclination to keep their gold and silver to themselves, had it been in any degree practicable.

But as any body of water may be raised above the level of the surrounding element, if the former has no communication with the latter; so in money, if the communication be cut off, by any material or physical impediment, (for all laws alone are ineffectual) there may, in such a case, be a very great inequality of money. Thus the immense distance of China, together with the monopolies of our India companies, obstructing the communication, preserve in Europe the gold and silver, especially the latter, in much greater plenty than they are found in that kingdom. But, notwithstanding this great obstruction, the force of the causes above mentioned is still evident. The skill and ingenuity of Europe in general surpasses perhaps that of China, with regard to manual arts and manufactures; yet are we never able to trade thither without great disadvantage. And were it not for the continual recruits, which we receive from America, money would soon sink in Europe, and

and rife in China, till it came nearly to a level in both places. Nor can any reasonable man doubt, but that induſtrious nation, were they as near us as Poland or Barbary, would drain us of the overplus of our ſpecie, and draw to themſelves a larger ſhare of the Weſt Indian treaſures. We need not have recourſe to a phyſical attraction, in order to explain the neceſſity of this operation. There is a moral attraction, ariſing from the intereſts and paſſions of men, which is full as potent and infallible.

How is the balance kept in the provinces of every kingdom among themſelves, but by the force of this principle, which makes it impoſſible for money to loſe its level, and either to riſe or ſink beyond the proportion of the labour and commodities which are in each province? Did not long experience make people eaſy on this head, what a fund of gloomy reflections might calculations afford to a melancholy Yorkſhireman, while he computed and magnified the ſums drawn to London by taxes, abſentees, commodities, and found on compariſon the oppoſite articles ſo much inferior? And no doubt, had the heptarchy ſubſiſted in England, the legiſlature of each ſtate had been continually alarmed by the fear of a wrong balance; and as it is probable that the mutual hatred of theſe ſtates would have been extremely violent on account of their cloſe neighbourhood,

hood, they would have loaded and oppreſſed all commerce, by a jealous and ſuperfluous caution. Since the union has removed the barriers between Scotland and England, which of theſe nations gains from the other by this free commerce? Or if the former kingdom has received any increaſe of riches, can it reaſonably be accounted for by any thing but the increaſe of its art and induſtry? It was a common apprehenſion in England, before the union, as we learn from L'Abbe du Bos*, that Scotland would ſoon drain them of their treaſure, were an open trade allowed; and on the other ſide the Tweed a contrary apprehenſion prevailed: with what juſtice in both, time has ſhown.

What happens in ſmall portions of mankind, muſt take place in greater. The provinces of the Roman empire, no doubt, kept their balance with each other, and with Italy, independent of the legiſlature: as much as the ſeveral counties of Britain, or the ſeveral pariſhes of each county. And any man who travels over Europe at this day, may ſee, by the prices of commodities, that money, in ſpite of the abſurd jealouſy of princes and ſtates, has brought itſelf nearly to a level; and that the difference between one kingdom and another is not greater in this reſpect, that it is often between different

---

* *Les interets d'*Angleterre *mal-entendus.*

rent provinces of the same kingdom. Men naturally flock to capital cities, sea-ports, and navigable rivers. There we find more men, more industry, more commodities, and consequently more money; but still the latter difference holds proportion with the former, and the level is preserved.

Our jealousy and our hatred of France are without bounds; and the former sentiment, at least, must be acknowledged reasonable and well-grounded. These passions have occasioned innumerable barriers and obstructions upon commerce, where we are accused of being commonly the aggressors. But what have we gained by the bargain? We lost the French market for our woollen manufactures, and transferred the commerce of wine to Spain and Portugal, where we buy worse liquor at a higher price. There are few Englishmen who would not think their country absolutely ruined, were French wines sold in England so cheap and in such abundance as to supplant, in some measure, all ale, and home-brewed liquors: But would we lay aside prejudice, it would not be difficult to prove, that nothing could be more innocent, perhaps advantageous. Each new acre of vineyard planted in France, in order to supply England with wine, would make it requisite for the French to take the produce

produce of an English acre, sown in wheat or barley, in order to subsist themselves; and it is evident, that we should thereby get command of the better commodity.

There are many edicts of the French King, prohibiting the planting of new vineyards, and ordering all those which are lately planted to be grubbed up: so sensible are they, in that country, of the superior value of corn, above every other product.

Mareschal Vauban complains often, and with reason, of the absurd duties which load the entry of those wines of Languedoc, Guienne, and other southern provinces, that are imported into Britanny and Normandy. He entertained no doubt but these latter provinces could preserve their balance, notwithstanding the open commerce which he recommends. And it is evident, that a few leagues more navigation to England would make no difference; or if it did, that it must operate alike on the commodities of both kingdoms.

There is indeed one expedient by which it is possible to sink, and another by which we may raise, money beyond its natural level in any kingdom; but these cases, when examined, will be found to resolve into our general theory, and to bring additional authority to it.

I scarcely know any method of sinking money below its level, but those institutions
of

of banks, funds, and paper-credit, which are so much practised in this kingdom. These render paper equivalent to money, circulate it through the whole state, make it supply the place of gold and silver, raise proportionably the price of labour and commodities, and by that means either banish a great part of those precious metals, or prevent their farther increase. What can be more short-sighted than our reasonings on this head? We fancy, because an individual would be much richer, were his stock of money doubled, that the same good effect would follow were the money of every one increased; not considering, that this would raise as much the price of every commodity, and reduce every man, in time, to the same condition as before. It is only in our public negotiations and transactions with foreigners, that a greater stock of money is advantageous; and as our paper is there absolutely insignificant, we feel, by its means, all the ill effects arising from a great abundance of money, without reaping any of the advantages. *

Suppose

---

* Money, when increasing, gives encouragement to industry, during the interval between the increase of money and rise of the prices. A good effect of this nature may follow too from paper-credit; but it is dangerous to precipitate matters, at the risk of losing all by the failing of that credit, as must happen upon any violent shock in public affairs.

Suppose that there are 12 millions of paper, which circulate in the kingdom as money, (for we are not to imagine, that all our enormous funds are employed in that shape) and suppose the real cash of the kingdom to be 18 millions: here is a state which is found by experience to be able to hold a stock of 30 millions. I say, if it be able to hold it, it must of necessity have acquired it in gold and silver, had we not obstructed the entrance of these metals by this new invention of paper. Whence would it have acquired that sum? From all the kingdoms of the world. But why? Because, if you remove these 12 millions, money in this state is below its level, compared with our neighbours; and we must immediately draw from all of them, till we be full and saturate, so to speak, and can hold no more. By our present politics, we are as careful to stuff the nation with this fine commodity of bank-bills and chequer-notes, as if we were afraid of being overburthened with the precious metals.

It is not to be doubted, but the great plenty of bullion in France is, in a great measure, owing to the want of paper-credit. The French have no banks: merchants bills do not there circulate as with us: usury or lending on interest is not directly permitted; so that many have large sums in their coffers: great quantities of plate are used

used in private houses; and all the churches are full of it. By this means, provisions and labour still remain cheaper among them, than in nations that are not half so rich in gold and silver. The advantages of this situation, in point of trade as well as in great public emergencies, are too evident to be disputed.

The same fashion a few years ago prevailed in Genoa, which still has place in England and Holland, of using services of China-ware instead of plate; but the senate, foreseeing the consequence, prohibited the use of that brittle commodity beyond a certain extent; while the use of silver-plate was left unlimited. And I suppose, in their late distresses, they felt the good effect of this ordinance. Our tax on plate is, perhaps, in this view, somewhat unpolitic.

Before the introduction of paper-money into our colonies, they had gold and silver sufficient for their circulation. Since the introduction of that commodity, the least inconveniency that has followed is the total banishment of the precious metals. And, after the abolition of paper, can it be doubted but money will return, while these colonies possess manufactures and commodities, the only thing valuable in commerce, and for whose sake alone all men desire money.

What pity Lycurgus did not think of paper-credit, when he wanted to banish gold

gold and silver from *Sparta!* It would have served his purpose better than the lumps of iron he made use of as money; and would also have prevented more effectually all commerce with strangers, as being of so much less real and intrinsic value.

It must, however, be confessed, that, as all these questions of trade and money are extremely complicated, there are certain lights, in which this subject may be placed, so as to represent the advantages of paper-credit and banks to be superior to their disadvantages. That they banish specie and bullion from a state is undoubtedly true; and whoever looks no farther than this circumstance, does well to condemn them; but specie and bullion are not of so great consequence as not to admit of a compensation, and even an overbalance from the increase of industry and of credit, which may be promoted by the right use of paper-money. It is well known of what advantage it is to a merchant to be able to discount his bills upon occasion; and every thing that facilitates this species of traffic is favourable to the general commerce of a state. But private bankers are enabled to give such credit by the credit they receive from the depositing of money in their shops; and the bank of England in the same manner, from the liberty it has to issue its notes in all payments. There was an invention of this kind,

kind, which was fallen upon some years ago by the banks of Edinburgh; and which, as it is one of the most ingenious ideas that has been executed in commerce, has also been thought advantageous to Scotland. It is there called a *bank-credit*; and is of this nature. A man goes to the bank and finds surety to the amount, we shall suppose, of five thousand pounds. This money, or any part of it, he has the liberty of drawing out whenever he pleases, and he pays only the ordinary interest for it, while it is in his hands. He may, when he pleases, repay any sum so small as twenty pounds, and the interest is discounted from the very day of the repayment. The advantages, resulting from this contrivance, are manifold. As a man may find surety nearly to the amount of his substance, and his bank-credit is equivalent to ready money, a merchant does hereby, in a manner, coin his houses, his houshold furniture, the goods in his warehouse, the foreign debts due to him, his ships at sea; and can, upon occasion, employ them in all payments, as if they were the current money of the country. If a man borrow five thousand pounds from a private hand, besides that it is not always to be found when required, he pays interest for it, whether he be using it or not: his bank-credit costs him nothing except during the very moment, in which it is of service to him:

him: And this circumstance is of equal advantage as if he had borrowed money at much lower interest. Merchants, likewise, from this invention, acquire a great facility in supporting each other's credit, which is a considerable security against bankruptcies. A man, when his own bank-credit is exhausted, goes to any of his neighbours who is not in the same condition; and he gets the money, which he replaces at his convenience.

After this practice had taken place, during some years, at Edinburgh, several companies of merchants at Glasgow carried the matter farther. They associated themselves into different banks, and issued notes so low as ten shillings, which they used in all payments for goods, manufactures, tradesmen's labour of all kinds; and these notes, from the established credit of the companies, passed as money in all payments throughout the country. By this means, a stock of five thousand pounds was able to perform the same operations as if it were six or seven; and merchants were thereby enabled to trade to a greater extent, and to require less profit in all their transactions. But whatever other advantages result from these inventions, it must still be allowed, that they banish the precious metals; and nothing can be a more evident proof of it, than a comparison of the past and present condition of Scotland in that particular. It was found, upon the re-

coinage

coinage made after the union, that there was near a million of specie in that country: but notwithstanding the great increase of riches, commerce, and manufactures of all kinds, it is thought, that, even where there is no extraordinary drain made by England, the current specie will not now amount to a third of that sum.

But as our projects of paper-credit are almost the only expedient, by which we can sink money below its level; so, in my opinion, the only expedient, by which we can raise money above it, is a practice which we should all exclaim against as destructive, namely, the gathering of large sums into a public treasure, locking them up, and absolutely preventing their circulation. The fluid, not communicating with the neighbouring element, may, by such an artifice, be raised to what height we please. To prove this, we need only return to our first supposition, of annihilating the half or any part of our cash; where we found, that the immediate consequence of such an event would be the attraction of an equal sum from all the neighbouring kingdoms. Nor does there seem to be any necessary bounds set, by the nature of things, to this practice of hoarding. A small city, like Geneva, continuing this policy for ages, might ingross nine-tenths of the money of Europe. There seems, indeed, in the nature of man, an invincible

vincible obstacle to that immense growth of riches. A weak state, with an enormous treasure, will soon become a prey to some of its poorer, but more powerful neighbours. A great state would dissipate its wealth in dangerous and ill-concerted projects; and probably destroy, with it, what is much more valuable, the industry, morals, and numbers of its people. The fluid, in this case, raised to too great a height, bursts and destroys the vessel that contains it; and mixing itself with the surrounding element, soon falls to its proper level.

So little are we commonly acquainted with this principle, that, though all historians agree in relating uniformly so recent an event, as the immense treasure amassed by Harry VII. (which they make amount to 2,700,000 pounds,) we rather reject their concurring testimony, than admit of a fact, which agrees so ill with our inveterate prejudices. It is indeed probable, that this sum might be three-fourths of all the money in England. But where is the difficulty in conceiving, that such a sum might be amassed in twenty years, by a cunning, rapacious, frugal, and almost absolute monarch? Nor is it probable, that the diminution of circulating money was ever sensibly felt by the people, or ever did them any prejudice. The sinking of the prices of all commodities would immediately replace it, by giving England

England the advantage in its commerce with the neighbouring kingdoms.

Have we not an inftance, in the fmall republic of Athens with its allies, who, in about fifty years, between the Median and Peloponnefian wars, amaffed a fum not much inferior to that of Harry VII.*? For all the Greek hiftorians † and orators ‡ agree, that the Athenians collected in the citadel more than 10,000 talents, which they afterwards diffipated to their own ruin, in rafh and imprudent enterprizes. But when this money was fet a running, and began to communicate with the furrounding fluid; what was the confequence? Did it remain in the ftate? No. For we find, by the memorable *cenfus* mentioned by Demofthenes ‖ and Polybius §, that, in about fifty years afterwards, the whole value of the republic, comprehending lands, houfes, commodities, flaves, and money, was lefs than 6000 talents.

What an ambitious high-fpirited people was this, to collect and keep in their treafury, with a view to conquefts, a fum, which it was every day in the power of the citizens, by a fingle vote, to diftribute among themfelves, and which would have gone near to triple the riches of every individual! For

---

* There were about eight ounces of filver in a pound fterling in Harry VII.'s time.

† Thucydides, lib. ii. and Diod. Sic. lib. xii.

‡ Vid. Æfchinis et Demofthenis Epift.

‖ Περι Συμμοριας. § Lib. ii. cap. 62.

we must observe, that the numbers and private riches of the Athenians are said, by ancient writers, to have been no greater at the beginning of the Peloponnesian war, than at the beginning of the Macedonian.

Money was little more plentiful in Greece during the age of Philip and Perseus, than in England during that of Harry VII. yet these two monarchs in thirty years * collected from the small kingdom of Macedon, a larger treasure than that of the English monarch. Paulus Æmilius brought to Rome about 1,700,000 pounds sterling †. Pliny says, 2,400,000 ‡. And that was but a part of the Macedonian treasure. The rest was dissipated by the resistance and flight of Perseus §.

We may learn from Stanian, that the canton of Berne had 300,000 pounds lent at interest, and had above six times as much in their treasury. Here then is a sum hoarded of 1,800,000 pounds sterling, which is at least quadruple what should naturally circulate in such a petty state; and yet no one, who travels in the Pais de Vaux, or any part of that canton, observes any want of money more than could be supposed in a country of that extent, soil, and situation. On the contrary, there are scarce any inland provinces on the continent of France or Germany where the inhabitants are at this time,

---

* Titi Livii, lib. xlv. cap. 40.   † Lib. xxxiii. cap. 3.
‡ Vel. Paterc. lib. i. cap. 9.   § Titi Livii, ibid.

so opulent, though that canton has vastly increased its treasure since 1714, the time when Stanian wrote his judicious account of Switzerland.*

The account given by Appian † of the treasure of the Ptolomies, is so prodigious, that one cannot admit of it; and so much the less, because the historian says, that the other successors of Alexander were also frugal, and had many of them treasures not much inferior. For this saving humour of the neighbouring princes must necessarily have checked the frugality of the Egyptian monarchs, according to the foregoing theory. The sum he mentions is 740,000 talents, or 191,166,666 pounds 13 shillings and 4 pence, according to Dr. Arburthnot's computation. And yet Appian says, that he extracted his account from the public records; and he was himself a native of Alexandria.

From these principles we may learn what judgment we ought to form of those numberless bars, obstructions, and imposts, which all nations of Europe, and none more than England, have put upon trade; from an exorbitant desire of amassing money, which never will heap up beyond its level, while it circulates;

---

* The poverty which Stanian speaks of is only to be seen in the most mountainous cantons, where there is no commodity to bring money: and even there the people are not poorer than in the diocese of Saltsburgh on the one hand, or Savoy on the other.

† Proem.

circulates; or from an ill-grounded apprehension of losing their specie, which never will sink below it. Could any thing scatter our riches, it would be such unpolitic contrivances. But this general ill effect, however, results from them, that they deprive neighbouring nations of that free communication and exchange which the author of the world has intended, by giving them soils, climates and geniuses, so different from each other.

Our modern politics embrace the only method of banishing money, the using of paper-credit; they reject the only method of amassing it, the practice of hoarding; and they adopt a hundred contrivances, which serve to no purpose but to check industry, and rob ourselves and our neighbours of the common benefits of art and nature.

All taxes, however, upon foreign commodities, are not to be regarded as prejudicial or useless, but those only which are founded on the jealousy above-mentioned. A tax on German linen encourages home manufactures, and thereby multiplies our people and industry. A tax on brandy encreases the sale of rum, and supports our southern colonies. And as it is necessary, that imposts should be levied, for the support of government, it may be thought more convenient to lay them on foreign commodities, which can easily be intercepted at the port, and subjected to the impost. We ought

ought however, always to rembember the maxim of Dr. Swift, that in the arithmetic of the cuſtoms, two and two make not four, but often make only one. It can ſcarcely be doubted, but if the duties on wine were lowered to a third, they would yield much more to the government than at preſent: our people might thereby afford to drink commonly a better and more wholeſome liquor; and no prejudice would enſue to the balance of trade, of which we are ſo jealous. The manufacture of ale beyond the agriculture is but inconſiderable, and gives employment to few hands. The tranſport of wine and corn would not be much inferior.

But are there not frequent inſtances, you will ſay, of ſtates and kingdoms, which were formerly rich and opulent, and are now poor and beggarly? Has not the money left them, with which they formerly abounded? I anſwer, if they loſe their trade, induſtry, and people, they cannot expect to keep their gold and ſilver: for theſe precious metals will hold proportion to the former advantages. When Liſbon and Amſterdam got the Eaſt-India trade from Venice and Genoa, thay alſo got the profits and money which aroſe from it. Where the ſeat of government is transferred, where expenſive armies are maintained at a diſtance, where great funds are poſſeſſed by foreigners; there naturally follows from theſe cauſes a diminution of the ſpecie. But theſe, we may obſerve, are violent and forcible

cible methods of carrying away money, and are in time commonly attended with the transport of people and industry. But where these remain, and the drain is not continued, the money always finds its way back again, by a hundred canals, of which we have no notion or suspicion. What immense treasures have been spent, by so many nations, in Flanders, since the revolution, in the course of three long wars? More money perhaps than the half of what is at present in Europe. But what has now become of it? Is it in the narrow compass of the Austrian provinces? No, surely: it has most of it returned to the several countries whence it came, and has followed that art and industry, by which at first it was acquired. For above a thousand years, the money of Europe has been flowing to Rome, by an open and sensible current; but it has been emptied by many secret and insensible canals: and the want of industry and commerce renders at present the papal dominions the poorest territory in all Italy.

In short, a government has great reason to preserve with care its people and its manufactures. Its money, it may safely trust to the course of human affairs, without fear or jealousy. Or if it ever give attention to this latter circumstance, it ought only to be so far as it affects the former.

Essay

ESSAY II.

On the JEALOUSY of TRADE.

HAVING endeavoured to remove one species of ill-founded jealousy, which is so prevalent among commercial nations, it may not be amiss to mention another, which seems equally groundless. Nothing is more usual, among states which have made some advances in commerce, than to look on the progress of their neighbours with a suspicious eye, to consider all trading states as their rivals, and to suppose that it is impossible for any of them to flourish, but at their expence. In opposition to this narrow and malignant opinion, I will venture to assert, that the increase of riches and commerce in any one nation, instead of hurting, commonly promote the riches and commerce of all its neighbours; and that a state can scarcely carry its trade and industry very far, where all the surrounding states are buried in ignorance, sloth, and barbarism.

It is obvious, that the domestic industry of a people cannot be hurt by the greatest prosperity of their neighbours; and as this branch of commerce is undoubtedly the most important in any extensive kingdom, we are so far removed from all reason of jealousy. But I go farther, and observe, that where an open communication is preserved among nations, it is impossible but the domestic industry of every one must receive an increase from the improvements of the others. Compare the situation of Great Britain, at present, with what it was two centuries ago. All the arts, both of agriculture and manufactures, were then extremely rude and imperfect. Every improvement, which we have since made, has arisen from our imitation of foreigners; and we ought so far to esteem it happy, that they had previously made advances in arts and ingenuity. But this intercourse is still upheld to our great advantage: notwithstanding the advanced state of our manufactures, we daily adopt, in every art, the inventions and improvements of our neighbours. The commodity is first imported from abroad, to our great discontent, while we imagine that it drains us of our money: afterwards, the art itself is gradually imported, to our visible advantage: yet we continue still to repine, that our neighbours should possess any art, industry, and invention; forgetting that, had they not first instructed us, we should have been, at present, barbarians; and did they not still continue their instructions, the arts must fall into a state of languor, and lose that emulation and novelty, which contribute so much to their advancement.

The encrease of domestic industry lays the foundation of foreign commerce. Where a
great

great number of commodities are raised and perfected for the home-market, there will always be found some which can be exported with advantage. But if our neighbours have no art or cultivation, they cannot take them; because they will have nothing to give in exchange. In this respect, states are in the same condition as individuals. A single man can scarcely be industrious, where all his fellow-citizens are idle. The riches of the several members of a community contribute to encrease my riches, whatever profession I may follow. They consume the produce of my industry, and afford me the produce of theirs in return.

Nor needs any state entertain apprehensions, that their neighbours will improve to such a degree in every art and manufacture, as to have no demand from them. Nature, by giving a diversity of geniuses, climates, and soils, to different nations, has secured their mutual intercourse and commerce, as long as they all remain industrious and civilized. Nay, the more the arts encrease in any state, the more will be its demands from its industrious neighbours. The inhabitants, having become opulent and skilful, desire to have every commodity in the utmost perfection; and as they have plenty of commodities to give in exchange, they make large importations from every foreign country. The industry of the nations, from whom they import, receives encouragement: their own

own is alfo increafed, by the fale of the commodities which they give in exchange.

But what if a nation has any ftaple commodity, fuch as the woollen manufactory is in England? Muft not the interfering of their neighbours in that manufacture be a lofs to them? I anfwer, that, when any commodity is denominated the ftaple of a kingdom, it is fuppofed that this kingdom has fome peculiar and natural advantages for raifing the commodity; and if, notwithftanding thefe advantages, they lofe fuch a manufactory, they ought to blame their own idlenefs, or bad government, not the induftry of their neighbours. It ought alfo to be confidered, that, by the increafe of induftry among the neighbouring nations, the confumption of every particular fpecies of commodity is alfo encreafed; and though foreign manufactures interfere with us in the market, the demand for our product may ftill continue, or even encreafe. And fhould it diminifh, ought the confequence to be efteemed fo fatal? If the fpirit of induftry be preferved, it may eafily be diverted from one branch to another; and the manufacturers of wool, for inftance, be employed in linen, filk, iron, or any other commodities, for which there appears to be a demand. We need not apprehend, that all the objects of induftry will be exhaufted, or that our manufacturers, while they remain on an equal footing with thofe of our neighbours, will be be in danger of wanting employment. The emulation among rival nations ferves rather to keep induftry alive in all of them: And any people is happier who poffefs a variety of manufactures, than if they enjoyed one fingle great manufacture, in which they are all employed. Their fituation is lefs precarious; and they will feel, lefs fenfibly, thofe revolutions and uncertainties, to which every particular branch of commerce will always be expofed.

The only commercial ftate, that ought to dread the improvements and induftry of their neighbours, is fuch a one as the Dutch, who, enjoying no extent of land, nor poffeffing any number of native commodities, flourifh only by their being the brokers, and factors, and carriers of others. Such a people may naturally apprehend, that, as foon as the neighbouring ftates come to know and purfue their intereft, they will take into their own hands the management of their affairs, and deprive their brokers of that profit, which they formerly reaped from it. But though this confequence may naturally be dreaded, it is very long before it takes place; and by art and induftry it may be warded off for many generations, if not wholly eluded. The advantage of fuperior ftocks and correfpondence is fo great, that it is not eafily overcome; and as all the tranfactions encreafe by the encreafe of induftry in the neighbouring ftates, even a people whofe commerce stands on this precarious basis, may at first reap a considerable profit from the flourishing condition of their neighbours. The Dutch, having mortgaged all their revenues, make not such a figure in political transactions as formerly; but their commerce is surely equal to what it was in the middle of the last century, when they were reckoned among the great powers of Europe.

Were our narrow and malignant politics to meet with success, we should reduce all our neighbouring nations to the same state of sloth and ignorance that prevails in Morocco and the coast of Barbary. But what would be the consequence? They could send us no commodities: they could take none from us: our domestic commerce itself would languish for want of emulation, example, and instruction: and we ourselves should soon fall into the same abject condition, to which we had reduced them. I shall therefore venture to acknowledge, that, not only as a man, but as a British subject, I pray for the flourishing commerce of Germany, Spain, Italy, and even France itself. I am at least certain, that Great-Britain, and all those nations, would flourish more, did their sovereigns and ministers adopt such enlarged and benevolent sentiments towards each other.

ESSAY III.

On the BALANCE of POWER.

IT is a question, whether the idea of the balance of power be owing intirely to modern policy, or whether the phrase only has been invented in these later ages? It is certain, that Xenophon,* in his Institution of Cyrus, represents the combination of the Asiatic powers to have arisen from a jealousy of the encreasing force of the Medes and Persians; and though that elegant composition should be supposed altogether romance, this sentiment, ascribed by the author to the eastern Princes, is at least a proof of the prevailing notion of ancient times.

In all the politics of Greece, the anxiety, with regard to the balance of power, is apparent, and is expressly pointed out to us, even by the ancient historians. Thucydides † represents the league, which was formed against Athens, and which produced the Peloponnesian war, as intirely owing to this principle. And after the decline of Athens, when the Thebans and Lacedemonians disputed for sovereignty, we find, that the Athenians (as well as many other republics) always threw themselves into the lighter scale, and endeavoured to preserve the balance.

* Lib. i.   † Lib. i.

lance. They supported Thebes against Sparta, till the great victory gained by Epaminondas at Leuctra; after which they immediately went over to the conquered, from generosity, as they pretended, but, in reality, from their jealousy of the conquerors.*

Whoever will read Demosthenes's oration for the Megalopolitans, may see the utmost refinements on this principle, that ever entered into the head of a Venetian or English speculatist. And upon the first rise of the Macedonian power, this orator immediately discovered the danger, sounded the alarm through all Greece, and at last assembled that confederacy under the banners of Athens, which fought the great and decisive battle of Chaeronea.

It is true, the Grecian wars are regarded by historians as wars of emulation rather than of politics; and each state seems to have had more in view the honour of leading the rest, than any well-grounded hopes of authority and dominion. If we consider, indeed, the small number of inhabitants in any one republic, compared to the whole, the great difficulty of forming sieges in those times, and the extraordinary bravery and discipline of every freeman among that noble people; we shall conclude, that the balance of power was, of itself, sufficiently secured in Greece, and needed not to have been guarded with that caution which may be requisite

* Xenoph. Hist. Graec. lib. vi. & vii.

quifite in other ages. But whether we afcribe the fhifting of fides in all the Grecian republics, to *jealous emulation,* or *cautious politics,* the effects were alike, and every prevailing power was fure to meet with a confederacy againft it, and that often compofed of its former friends and allies.

The fame principle, call it envy or prudence, which produced the *Oſtracifm* of Athens, and *Petalifm* of Syracufe, and expelled every citizen whofe fame or power overtopped the reft; the fame principle, I fay, naturally difcovered itfelf in foreign politics, and foon raifed enemies to the leading ftate, however moderate in the exercife of its authority.

The Perfian monarch was really, in his force, a petty prince, compared to the Grecian republics; and therefore it behoved him, from views of fafety more than from emulation, to intereft himfelf in their quarrels, and to fupport the weaker fide in every conteft. This was the advice given by Alcibiedes to Tiffaphernes,* and it prolonged near a century the date of the Perfian empire; 'till the neglect of it for a moment, after the firft appearance of the afpiring genius of Philip, brought that lofty and frail edifice to the ground, with a rapidity of which there are few inftances in the hiftory of mankind.

The fucceffors of Alexander fhowed great jealoufy

* Thucyd. lib. viii.

jealousy of the balance of power; a jealousy founded on true politics and prudence, and which preserved distinct for several ages the partitions made after the death of that famous conqueror. The fortune and ambition of Antigonus * threatened them anew with an universal monarchy; but their combination, and their victory at Ipsus, saved them. And in after times, we find, that, as the eastern Princes considered the Greeks and Macedonians as the only real military force, with whom they had any intercourse, they kept always a watchful eye over that part of the world. The Ptolemies, in particular, supported first Aratus and the Achaeans, and then Cleomenes King of Sparta, from no other view than as a counterbalance to the Macedonian monarchs. For this is the account which Polybius gives of the Egyptian politics. †

The reason, why it is supposed, that the ancients were entirely ignorant of the balance of power, seems to be drawn from the Roman history more than the Grecian; and as the transactions of the former are generally the most familiar to us, we have thence formed all our conclusions. It must be owned, that the Romans never met with any such general combination or confederacy against them, as might naturally have been expected from their rapid conquest and declared ambition; but were allowed peaceably

ably to subdue their neighbours, one after another, till they extended their dominion over the whole known world. Not to mention the fabulous history of their Italic wars; there was, upon Hannibal's invasion of the Roman state, a remarkable crisis, which ought to have called up the attention of all civilized nations. It appeared afterwards (nor was it difficult to be observed at the time)† that this was a contest for universal empire; and yet no prince or state seems to have been in the least alarmed about the event or issue of the quarrel. Philip of Macedon remained neuter, till he saw the victories of Hannibal; and then most imprudently formed an alliance with the conqueror, upon terms still more imprudent. He stipulated, that he was to assist the Carthaginian state in their conquest of Italy; after which they engaged to send over forces into Greece, to assist him in subduing the Grecian commonwealths ‡.

The Rhodian and Achaen republics are much celebrated by antient historians for their wisdom and sound policy; yet both of them assisted the Romans in their wars against Philip and Antiochus. And what may be esteemed still a stronger proof, that this maxim

M

---

† It was observed by some, as appears by the speech of Agelaus of Naupactum, in the general congress of Greece. See Polyb. lib. v. cap. 104.

‡ Titi Livii, lib. xxiii. cap. 33.

maxim was not generally known in those ages; no ancient author has remarked the imprudence of these measures, nor has even blamed that absurd treaty above-mentioned made by Philip with the Carthaginians. Princes and statesmen, in all ages, may, before-hand, be blinded in their reasonings with regard to events: but it is somewhat extraordinary, that historians, afterwards, should not form a sounder judgment of them.

Massinissa, Attalus, Prusias, in gratifying their private passions, were, all of them, the instruments of the Roman greatness; and never seem to have suspected, that they were forging their own chains, while they advanced the conquests of their ally. A simple treaty and agreement between Massinissa and the Carthaginians, so much required by mutual interest, barred the Romans from all entrance into Africa, and preserved liberty to mankind.

The only Prince we meet with in the Roman history, who seems to have understood the balance of power, is Hiero King of Syracuse. Though the ally of Rome, he sent assistance to the Carthaginians, during the war of the auxiliaries; "Esteeming it requisite," says Polybius†, "both in order to "retain his dominions in Sicily, and to pre- "serve the Roman friendship, that Carthage "should

† Lib. i. cap. 83.

"should be safe; lest by its fall the remain-
"ing power should be able, without contrast
"or opposition, to execute every purpose and
"undertaking. And here he acted with
"great wisdom and prudence. For that is
"never, on any account, to be overlooked;
"nor ought such a force ever to be thrown
"into one hand, as to incapacitate the neigh-
"bouring states from defending their rights
"against it." Here is the aim of modern
politics pointed out in express terms.

In short, the maxim of preserving the balance of power is founded so much on common sense and obvious reasoning, that it is impossible it could altogether have escaped antiquity, where we find, in other particulars, so many marks of deep penetration and discernment. If it was not so generally known and acknowledged as at present, it had, at least, an influence on all the wiser and more experienced Princes and politicians. And indeed, even at present, however generally known and acknowledged among speculative reasoners, it has not, in practice, an authority much more extensive among those who govern the world.

After the fall of the Roman empire, the form of government, established by the northern conquerors, incapacitated them, in a great measure, for farther conquests, and long maintained each state in its proper boundaries. But when vassalage and the feudal militia were abolished, mankind were anew alarmed by the danger of universal monarchy, from the union of so many kingdoms and principalities in the person of the Emperor Charles. But the power of the house of Austria, founded on extensive but divided dominions, and their riches, derived chiefly from mines of gold and silver, were more likely to decay, of themselves, from internal defects, than to overthrow all the bulwarks raised against them. In less than a century, the force of that violent and haughty race was shattered, their opulence dissipated, their splendor eclipsed. A new power succeeded, more formidable to the liberties of Europe, possessing all the advantages of the former, and labouring under none of its defects; except a share of that spirit of bigotry and persecution, with which the house of Austria was so long, and still is so much infatuated.

In the general wars, maintained against this ambitious power, Britain has stood foremost; and she still maintains her station. Beside her advantages of riches and situation, her people are animated with such a national spirit, and are so fully sensible of the blessings of their government, that we may hope their vigour never will languish in so necessary and so just a cause. On the contrary, if we may judge by the past, their passionate ardour

dour seems rather to require some moderation; and they have oftener erred from a laudable excess than from a blameable deficiency.

In the first place, we seem to have been more possessed with the ancient Greek spirit of jealous emulation, that actuated by the prudent views of modern politics. Our wars with France have been begun with justice, and even, perhaps, from necessity; but have always been too far pushed from obstinacy and passion. The same peace, which was afterwards made at Ryswick in 1697, was offered so early as the year ninety-two; that concluded at Utrecht in 1712 might have been finished on as good conditions at Gertruytenberg in the year eight; and we might have given at Frankfort, in 1723, the same terms which we were glad to accept of at Aix-la-Chapelle in the year forty-eight. Here, then, we see, that above half of our wars with France, and all our public debts, are owing more to our own imprudent vehemence, than to the ambition of our neighbours.

In the second place, we are so decleared in our opposition to French power, and so alert in defence of our allies, that they always reckon upon our force as upon their own; and expecting to carry on war at our expence, refuse all reasonable terms of accommodation. *Habent subjectos, tanquam suos;*

suos; viles, ut alienos. All the world knows, that the factious vote of the House of Commons, in the beginning of the last Parliament, with the professed humour of the nation, made the Queen of Hungary inflexible in her terms, and prevented that agreement with Prussia, which would immediately have restored the general tranquility of Europe.

In the third place, we are such true combatants, that, when once engaged, we lose all concern for ourselves and our posterity, and consider only how we may best annoy the enemy. To mortgage our revenues at so deep a rate, in wars, where we were only accessories, was surely the most fatal delusion, that a nation, which had any pretension to politics or prudence, has ever yet been guilty of. That remedy of funding, if it be a remedy, and not rather a poison, ought, in all reason, to be reserved to the last extremity; and no evil, but the greatest and most urgent, should ever induce us to embrace so dangerous an expedient.

These excesses, to which we have been carried, are prejudicial; and may, perhaps, in time, become still more prejudicial another way, by begetting, as is usual, the opposite extreme, and rendering us totally careless and supine with regard to the fate of Europe. The Athenians, from the most bustling, intriguing, warlike people of Greece,

finding

finding their error in thrusting themselves into every quarrel, abandoned all attention to foreign affairs; and in no contest ever took part on either side, except by their flatteries and complaisance to the victor.

Enormous monarchies are, probably, destructive to human nature; in their progress, in their continuance,* and even in their downfal, which never can be very distant from their establishment. The military genius, which aggrandized the monarchy, soon leaves the court, the capital, and the center of such a government; while the wars are carried on at a great distance, and interest so small a part of the state. The antient nobility, whose affections attach them to their Sovereign, live all at court; and never will accept of military employments, which would carry them to remote and barbarous frontiers, where they are distant both from their pleasures and their fortune. The arms of the state, must, therefore, be entrusted to mercenary strangers, without zeal, without attachment, without honour; ready on every occasion to turn them against the prince, and join each desperate malcontent, who offers pay and plunder. This is the necessary progress of human affairs: thus human nature checks

* If the Roman empire was of advantage, it could only proceed from this, that mankind were generally in a very disorderly, uncivilized condition, before its establishment.

checks itself in its airy elevations: thus ambition blindly labours for the distruction of the conqueror, of his family, and of every thing near and dear to him. The Bourbons, trusting to the support of their brave, faithful, and affectionate nobility, would push their advantage, without reserve or limitation. These, while fired with glory and emulation, can bear the fatigues and dangers of war; but never would submit to languish in the garrisons of Hungary or Lithuania, forgot at court, and sacrificed to the intrigues of every minion or mistress, who approaches the Prince. The troops are filled with Cravates and Tartars, Hussars and Cossacks; intermingled, perhaps, with a few soldiers of fortune from the better provinces: and the melancholy fate of the Roman emperors, from the same cause, is renewed over and over again, 'till the final dissolution of the monarchy.

NEW BOOKS printed for JOHN STOCK-DALE, opposite *Burlington-house, Piccadilly.*

1. ARTICLES exhibited by the Knights, Citizens, and Burgesses in Parliament assembled, in the Name of themselves and of all the Commons of Great Britain, against WARREN HASTINGS, Esq. late Governor General of Bengal, in maintenance of their Impeachment against him for High Crimes and Misdemeanors (WITH THE AMENDMENTS). Price 2s. 6d.

2. The Answer of Warren Hastings, Esq. to the Articles exhibited by the Knights, Citizens, and Burgesses in Parliament assembled, in the Name of themselves, and of all the Commons of Great Britain, in maintenance of their Impeachment against him for High Crimes and Misdemeanors, supposed to have been by him committed. Delivered at the Bar of the House of Peers, on Wednesday, November 28, 1787. In One Volume 8vo. Price only 4s. in Boards.

3. Articles of Charge of High Crimes and Misdemeanors against Warren Hastings, Esq. presented to the House of Commons by the Right Hon. Edmund Burke. Also

4. The Defence of Warren Hastings, Esq. (late Governor General of Bengal), at the Bar of the House of Commons, upon the Matter of the several Charges of High Crimes and Misdemeanors, presented against him in the Year 1786. In one Volume 8vo. Price 10s. 6d. in Boards.

5. Minutes of the Evidence taken before a Committee of the House of Commons, being a Committee of the Whole House, appointed to consider of the several Articles of Charge of High Crimes and Misdemeanors presented to the House against Warren Hastings, Esq. late Governor General of Bengal: Containing the Examinations of Sir Robert Barker, Bart. Colonel Champion; Major Marsack; Captain Leonard Jaques; Major

Major Balfour; Major Gardener; Major Gilpin; Nathaniel Middleton, Efq. Captain Williams; Sir Elijah Impey; Captain Thomas Mercer; William Young, Efq. Mr. Ifaac Baugh; William Harwood, Efq. Ewan Law, Efq. Alexander Higginfon, Efq. Peter Moore, Efq. William Markham, Efq. David Anderfon, Efq. and Mr. William Wright. In one large Volume 8vo. Price 7s. 6d. in Boards.

6. Minutes of Warren Haftings and Philip Francis, Efquires, relative to their perfonal Quarrel. Price 1s. 6d.

7. The Indian Vocabulary of Perfian, Bengal, Turkifh, and Arabic Words, which occur in the Articles againft Mr. Haftings and his Anfwers, alfo in the different Reports, Books, and Papers, on Eaft-India Affairs; together with Explanations of the Names of certain Offices, and other local Expreffions contained in the fame: Revifed and corrected by feveral Gentlemen diftinguifhed for their Knowledge of the Oriental Languages. To which is prefixed the Forms of Impeachments. Neatly printed in a Pocket Volume. Price 3s. 6d.

8. Articles of Charge of High Crimes and Mifdemeanors, againft Sir Elijah Impey, Knt. late Chief Juftice of the Supreme Court of Judicature at Fort William, in Bengal, prefented to the Houfe of Commons, upon the 12th Day of December 1787, by Sir Gilbert Elliot, Bart. Price 2s. 6d.

9. The Tribunal, addreffed to the Peers of Great Britain fitting in Judgment on Warren Haftings. Price 2s. 6d.

10. Reflections on Impeaching and Impeachers: Addreffed to Warren Haftings, Efq. Price 1s.

11. A Review of the principal Charges againft Warren Haftings, Efq; late Governor General of Bengal. Price 2s. 6d.

12. A Letter to Philip Francis, Efq; from the Right Hon. Emund Burke, Chairman; Right Hon. C. J. Fox, R. B. Sheridan, Efq; Thomas Pelham, Efq; W. Windham,

ham, Esq; Sir G. Elliot, Bart. Charles Grey, Esq; William Adam, Esq; John Anstruther, Esq; Michael Ang. Taylor, Esq; Lord Maitland, Dudley Long, Esq; John Burgoyne, Esq; G. Aug. North, Esq; St. And. St. John, Esq; Richard Fitzpatrick, Esq; Roger Wilbraham, Esq; John Courtenay, Esq; Sir James Erskine, Bart. Members of the Committee for managing the Impeachment of Mr. Hastings; with Remarks. Price 1s.

13. The Impeachment, a Mock Heroic Poem. Price 1s. 6d.

14. The Bengal Calendar, for the Year 1788: Including a List of the Hon. and United East India Company's Civil and Military Servants on the Bengal Establishment, &c. Including also those at Madras, Bombay, Fort Marlborough, China, and St. Helena. A new Edition. Corrected at the East India House. Price 1s. 6d. sewed in Marble Paper.

15. The London Calendar, or Court and City Register for England, Scotland, Ireland, and America, for the Year 1788; including a complete and correct List of the present Parliament, &c. &c. &c. more extensive and useful than in any other Book of the Kind yet published. Carefully corrected at the respective Offices. Printed on a large Paper. Price only 1s. 6d. sewed, or 2s. bound.

☞ The above Calendar may be had complete with the New Heraldry in Miniature, containing the Arms of the Peers and Baronets: Almanack, Companion, and Bengal Calendar, bound together. Price 8s.

N. B. Be careful to ask for the London Calendar.

16. Fielding's New Peerage of England, Scotland, and Ireland for 1788; containing the Origin and Progress of Honours, Manner of creating Peers, Order of Knighthood, Introduction to Heraldry, with an Heraldic Dictionary, and a complete Extinct Peerage. In a neat Pocket Volume. Price only 6s. in Boards, or 7s. 6d Calf gilt.

⁎ The above new Edition of the Peerage is corrected to the present Time, and contains of Copper-plate and Letter-press 400 Pages, which is nearly double the

(4)

Quantity of the laſt Edition, though the Price is not advanced to the Public.

17. New Heraldry in Miniature: Containing all the Arms, Creſts, Supporters, and Mottos, of the Peers, Peereſſes, and Biſhops, of England, Scotland, and Ireland, with the Baronets of Great Britain; and the Inſignia of the different Orders of Knighthood in the Three Kingdoms: alſo an Introduction to the Science of Heraldry, a Dictionary of Heraldic Terms, as well as an Index to all the Peers, &c. with the Tranſlation of their Mottos: Likewiſe a Liſt of Titles conferred by his preſent Majeſty, and thoſe extinct ſince his Acceſſion to the Throne. Containing upwards of 1000 Arms of the Peers and Baronets, and Rules of Precedency amongſt Men and Women. Price only 2s. 6d. ſewed in Marble Paper.

18. The preſent State of the Eaſt Indies: By Warren Haſtings, Eſq; late Governor General of Bengal; with Notes by the Editor. Price only 2s.

19. A Tranſlation of the Memoirs of Eradut Khan, a Nobleman of Hindoſtan; containing intereſting Anecdotes of the Emperor Aumulgeer Aurungzebe, and of his Succeſſors, Shaw Aulum and Jehaunder Shaw: in which are diſplayed the Cauſes of the very precipitate Decline of the Mogul Empire in India. By Jonathan Scott, Captain in the Service of the Honourable Eaſt India Company, and private Perſian Tranſlator to Warren Haſtings, Eſq; late Governor General of Bengal, &c. 4to. 4s. 6d. Boards.

20. A Narrative of the Inſurrection which happened in the Zemeedary of Benares, in the Month of Auguſt, 1781, and of the Tranſactions in that Diſtrict; with an Appendix of authentic Papers and Affidavits. By Warren Haſtings, Eſq.

21. The Debate on the Rohilla War, in the Houſe of Commons, the 1ſt and 2d of June 1786. Price 1s. 6d.

22. The Debate on the Charge relative to Mr. Haſtings's Conduct to Cheyt Sing, at Benares, in the Houſe of Commons, on the 13h of June 1786. Price 1s.

23. The Debate in the Houſe of Commons, June 25th, 1786,

1786, on the East India Relief Bill, in which is included the History of the Diamond delivered to Lord Sydney by Major John Scott. Price 1s.

24. Remarks upon Col. Fullarton's View of the English Interests in India. Dedicated to the Officers in the Service of the East India Company in Bengal. By an Officer, late in the Company's Service in Bengal. Price 1s. 6d.

25. The Debates of the Last Session of the late Parliament, in Six Volumes, 8vo. Price 1l. 11s. 6d. half bound and lettered.

☞ The above Six Volumes contain Mr. Pitt's and Mr. Fox's East India Bills, and all the Debates on that Subject.

26. Also the Debates for 1784, First Session of the present Parliament (being the 16th), in Three large Volumes, 8vo. Price 1l. 1s. half bound and lettered.

27. Ditto 1785, Second Session, in Three Volumes, 8vo. Price 1l. 1s. half bound and lettered.

28. Debates in Parliament in 1786, Third Session, in Three Volumes, 8vo. Price 1l. 1s. half bound and lettered.

29. Ditto 1787, Fourth Session, in Three Volumes, 8vo. Price 1l. 1s. half bound and lettered.

☞ The above Debates contain a very full Account of the Proceedings respecting Mr. Hastings, and the East India Affairs.

30. Parliamentary Guide; or, Members' and Electors' complete Companion: being an historical Account of the several Cities, Counties, and Boroughs in Great Britain; their Right of Election; when they were first represented in Parliament, and the Number of Voters at each Place; with References to the Journals of the House of Commons, for every Proceeding to be found in them, relating to Matters of Election, and Copies of the several Writs used at a General Re-election; the Oaths taken by the Electors and the Elected; and the Oaths administered to the Representative upon taking his Seat, with a brief Recitation of all the various Statutes relating to the Election of Members; and the Succession of Parliaments from the

Restoration. In One large Volume, 8vo. Price 7s. in Boards.

31. The Resolves of the Committee appointed to try the Merits of the Election for the County of Glocester, in the Year 1777. George Berkley, Esq; Petitioner. William Bromley Chester, Esq; sitting Member. By Sir Cecil Wray, Bart. In One Volume, 8vo. Price 4s. in Boards.

32. The Works of Dr. Samuel Johnson. Volumes the 12th, 13th, and 14th. Price 19s. in Boards.

33. Also the Works of Dr. Johnson, complete. In Fourteen Volumes. Price 4l. 5s. in Boards, or elegantly Calf gilt, 5l. 6s.

☞ The Twelfth and Thirteenth Volumes may be had separate. Price 12s. in Boards.

*** The Publisher particularly requests those Gentlemen who intend to complete Johnson's Works, will do it as soon as possible, otherwise they may not have an Opportunity; as there are but few remaining.

34. The Gentleman's Magazine complete, from 1731 to 1786, inclusive, 60 Volumes, half bound and uniform; very scarce.

35. Poems on various Subjects. By Henry James Pye, Esq. M. P. Elegantly printed in Two Vols. 8vo. and embellished with beautiful Frontispieces. Price 12s. in Boards.

36. A Collection of Original Royal Letters, written by King Charles the First and Second, King James the Second, and the King and Queen of Bohemia. Together with Original Letters, written by Prince Rupert, Charles Louis Count Palatine, the Duchess of Hanover, and several other distinguished Persons, from the Year 1619 to 1665. Dedicated with Permission to his Majesty. By Sir George Bromley, Bart. (Ornamented with elegant Engravings, from original Paintings by Cooper, Sir Peter Lely, &c. executed by Messrs. Sherwins, of the Queen of Bohemia, Emanuel Scrope Howe, Prince Rupert, and Ruperta, natural Daughter of Prince Rupert; and a Plate of Autographs and Seals.) In One Volume. Price 10s. 6d. in Boards.

37. Stock-

37. Stockdale's Edition of Shakefpeare; including, in One Volume, 8vo. the whole of his Dramatic Works; with Explanatory Notes, compiled from various Commentators. To which are prefixed his Life and Will. Price only 15s.

☞ Gentlemen in the Country finding a Difficulty in procuring the above valuable Work, by directing a Line to Mr. Stockdale, oppofite Burlington-houfe, Piccadilly (appointing the Payment thereof in London), fhall have it immediately forwarded (Carriage paid) to any Part of Great Britain.

38. Philofophical and Critical Enquiries concerning Chriftianity. By Monfieur Charles Bonnet, of Geneva, F. R. S. Member of the Royal Academy of Sciences of Paris, &c. &c. Tranflated from the French by John Lewis Boiffier, Efq. (Ornamented with an elegant Engraving of the Author, by Sherwin, and neatly printed in 1 Vol. 8vo. Price 6s. in Boards.)

39. Sermons on important and interefting Subjects. By the Rev. Percival Stockdale. Illuftrated with an elegant Engraving of the Author. Price 6s. in Boards.

40. The Hiftory of New Holland, from its firft Difcovery in 1616, to the prefent Time, with a particular Account of its Produce and Inhabitants, and a Defcription of Botany Bay. Alfo a Lift of the Naval, Marine, Military and Civil Eftablifhment. Illuftrated with a large Map of New Holland, a Chart of Botany Bay, and a General Chart from England to Botany Bay, neatly coloured. To which is prefixed, an Introductory Difcourfe on Banifhment. By the Right Hon. William Eden. In 1 Vol. 8vo. Price 6s. in Boards.

41. The Hiftory of the Union between England and Scotland; with a Collection of Original Papers relating thereto. By the celebrated Daniel de Foe. With an Introduction, in which the Confequences and Probability of a like Union between this Country and Ireland are confidered, by John Lewis de Lolme, Author of the Work on the Conftitution of England. To which is prefixed a Life of the Author, and a copious Index. In One large Volume

(8)

Quarto, containing One Thousand Pages, with an elegant Engraving of the Author. Price 1l. 10s. in Boards.

☞ The Union between England and Scotland, being an extremely interesting Event, has led the Publisher to imagine, that a new Edition of this Work of De Foe, which is grown very scarce, would be acceptable to the Public, especially at the present Time, when the Situation of Affairs in Ireland induces many Persons to wish that a similar Union between Great Britain and that Kingdom may take place, as it may cause such an Union, if not to be effected, at least to be proposed, and to become, for a Time, the Subject of Debate in both Countries.

42. Historical Tracts. By Sir John Davies, Attorney-General, and Speaker of the House of Commons in Ireland; consisting of, 1. A Discovery of the true Cause why Ireland was never brought under Obedience to the Crown of England. 2. A Letter to the Earl of Salisbury, on the State of Ireland in 1607. 3. A Letter to the Earl of Salisbury in 1610, giving an Account of the Plantation in Ulster. 4. A Speech to the Lord Deputy in 1613, tracing the ancient Constitution of Ireland. To which is prefixed, a new Life of the Author, from authentic Documents. In One Volume Octavo, Price 5s. in Boards, or 6s. in Calf and lettered.

*** The above Work is spoken of by Mr. De Lolme, in the highest Terms, in his Essay on the Union.

43. The Beauties of the British Senate; taken from the Debates of the Lords and Commons, from the Beginning of the Administration of Sir Robert Walpole, to the End of the Second Session of the Right Honourable William Pitt. Being an impartial Selection of, or faithful Extracts from, the most eminent Speeches, delivered in the Course of a most important and truly interesting Period, of more than Sixty Years, severally arranged under their respective Heads, with the Names of the Members, to whom they are attributed, annexed thereto. To which is prefixed, The Life of Sir Robert Walpole. In Two Volumes, Octavo.

(9)

Octavo. Price 10s. 6d. in Boards, or 12s. bound in Calf and lettered.

44. Debates in Parliament. By Dr. Samuel Johnson. In Two Volumes, 8vo. Price 12s. in Boards.

45. Four Tracts. By Thomas Day, Esq. In One Volume, 8vo. Price 10s. 6d.

46. A Complete Geographical Dictionary; or, Universal Gazetteer, of Antient and Modern Geography: containing a full, particular, and accurate Description of the known World in Europe, Asia, Africa, and America; comprising a complete System of Geography, illustrated with correct Maps and beautiful Views of the principal Cities, &c. and Chronological Tables of the Sovereigns of Europe. The Geographical Parts by John Scally, A. M. Member of the Roman Academy; Author of the Histoire Chronologique, sacrée et profane; Elements of Geography and Astronomy, &c. &c. interspersed with Extracts from the private Manuscripts of one of the Officers who accompanied Captain Cook in his Voyage to the Southern Hemisphere. The Astronomical Parts from the Papers of the late Mr. Israel Lyons, of Cambridge, Astronomer in Lord Mulgrave's Voyage to the Northern Hemisphere. In Two large Volumes, Quarto, bound in Calf, gilt, and lettered, Price 2l. 2s.

47. Godwin's Lives of the Bishops. By Richard. Illustrated with Seventy Copper-plates, and a beautiful Engraving of Godwin, by Virtu. In One large Volume, Folio, Price only 8s. 6d. in Boards.

48. History of Virginia. By his Excellency Thomas Jefferson, Minister Plenipotentiary from the United States to the Court of France. Illustrated with a large Map, comprehending the whole of Virginia, Maryland, Delaware, and Pennsylvania, and Parts of several other of the United States of America. In One Volume Octavo. Price 7s. in Boards.

49. The History of the Revolution of South Carolina. By David Ramsey, M. D. Illustrated with a large Map of South Carolina, and Parts adjacent, shewing the Movements

ments of the British and American Armies, together with several other Plans, shewing the Disposition and Stations of the Fleets and Armies. In Two large Volumes, 8vo. Price 12s. in Boards.

50. The Constitutions of the several Independent States of America; with a Preface and Dedication to the Duke of Portland. By the Reverend William Jackson. In One Vol. 8vo. Price 6s. in Boards.

51. Considerations on the present Situation of Great Britain, and her Commercial Connections. By Richard Champion, Esq. In One Volume, 8vo. Price 5s. in Boards.

52. An Estimate of the Comparative Strength of Great Britain, during the present and four preceding Reigns, and of the Losses of her Trade from every War since the Revolution. By George Chalmers, Esq. Price 3s. 6d. sewed, or 5s. Calf lettered.

53. An Essay containing Strictures on the Union of Scotland with England, and on the present Situation of Ireland; being an Introduction to De Foe's History of the Union. By J. L. De Lolme, Adv. Price 3s. 6d. sewed, containing 95 Pages in Quarto.

54. A brief Essay on the Advantages and Disadvantages which respectively attend France and Great Britain with regard to Trade. By Josiah Tucker, D. D. Dean of Gloucester. Price 2s.

55. Captain Cook's Third and last Voyage to the Pacific Ocean in the Years 1776, 1777, 1778, 1779, and 1780. Faithfully abridged from the Quarto Edition, published by Order of his Majesty; illustrated with Copper-plates. Price 4s. bound.

56. Stockdale's Edition of Shakspeare: including, in One Volume 8vo, the whole of his Dramatic Works; with Explanatory Notes, compiled from various Commentators; to which are prefixed, his Life and Will.

" Nature her Pencil to his Hand commits,
" And then in all her Forms to this great Master sits."

Price only 15s. in Boards; or elegantly Calf gilt, 18s.

(11)

ADDRESS TO THE PUBLIC.

A New Edition of Shakſpeare, and an Edition of ſo ſingular a Form as the preſent, in which all his Plays are comprehended in One Volume, will perhaps appear ſurpriſing to many Readers; but, upon a little Reflection, their Surpriſe will, the Editor doubts not, be converted into Approbation.

Much as Shakſpeare has been read of late Years, and largely as the Admiration and Study of him have been extended, there are ſtill a numerous Claſs of Men to whom he is very imperfectly known. Many of the middling and lower Ranks of the Inhabitants of this Country are either not acquainted with him at all, excepting by Name, or have only ſeen a few of his Plays, which have accidentally fallen in their Way. It is to ſupply the Wants of theſe Perſons that the preſent Edition is principally undertaken; and it cannot fail of becoming to them a perpetual Source of Entertainment and Inſtruction.

But the Inſtruction that may be drawn from Shakſpeare is equal to the Entertainment which his Writings afford. He is the greateſt Maſter of Human Nature, and of Human Life, that perhaps ever exiſted; ſo that we cannot peruſe his Works without having our Underſtandings conſiderably enlarged. To promote, therefore, the Knowledge of him is to contribute to general Improvement.

Nor is the Utility of the preſent Publication confined to Perſons of the Rank already deſcribed; it will be found ſerviceable even to thoſe whoſe Situation in Life hath enabled them to purchaſe all the expenſive Editions of our great Dramatiſt. The Book now offered to the Public may commodiouſly be taken into a Coach or a Poſt-chaiſe, for Amuſement in a Journey. It is a Compendium, not an Abridgment, of the nobleſt of our Poets, and a Library in a ſingle Volume.

The Editor hath endeavoured to give all the Perfection to this Work which the Nature of it will admit. The Account of his Life, which is taken from Rowe, and his Laſt Will, in reality comprehend almoſt every Thing that is known with regard to the perſonal Hiſtory of Shakſpeare.

The

The Notes which are subjoined are such as were necessary for the Purpose of illustrating and explaining obsolete Words, unusual Phrases, old Customs, and obscure or distant Allusions. In short, it has been the Editor's Aim to omit nothing which may serve to render Shakspeare intelligible to every Capacity, and to every Class of Readers.

Gentlemen in the Country finding a Difficulty in procuring the above valuable Work, by directing a Line to Mr. Stockdale, opposite Burlington-house, Piccadilly, (appointing the Payment thereof in London) shall have it immediately forwarded (Carriage paid) to any Part of Great Britain.

57. Essays on Hunting: containing a Philosophical Enquiry into the Nature and Properties of the Scent; and Observations on the different Kinds of Hounds, with the Manner of training them. Also, Directions for the Choice of a Hunter; the Qualifications requisite for a Huntsman; and other General Rules to be observed in every Contingency incident to the Chace. With an Introduction, describing the Method of Hare Hunting, practised by the Greeks. A new Edition: With a Supplement, containing an Account of the Vizier's Manner of Hunting in the Mogul Empire. By William Blane, Esq. In one Volume 8vo. Price 4s. in Boards.

58. The Letters of an Englishman, in which the Principles and Conduct of the Rockingham Party, when in Administration, and Opposition, are freely and impartially displayed. Price 2s. 6d.

59. The Letters of a Friend to the Rockingham Party in Answer to the above. Price 2s.

60. Silva, or a Discourse of Forest Trees; and the Propagation of Timber in his Majesty's Dominions. By John Evelyn Esq. With Notes by Dr. Hunter; with a fine Portrait of Evelyn, by Bartolozzi, in One large Volume Quarto. Price 2l. 12s. 6d. in Boards.

61. Georgical Essays. By Dr. A. Hunter. In One Volume Octavo. Price 7s. in Boards.

62. The Vision of Columbus, a Poem; in Nine Books. By Joel Barlow Esq. Price 3s. 6d. bound.

www.ingramcontent.com/pod-product-compliance
Lightning Source LLC
Chambersburg PA
CBHW020147170426
43199CB00010B/924